Rita Francis Mosscockle

Fantasias

Rita Francis Mosscockle

Fantasias

ISBN/EAN: 9783744752879

Printed in Europe, USA, Canada, Australia, Japan

Cover: Foto ©Thomas Meinert / pixelio.de

More available books at **www.hansebooks.com**

FANTASIAS

BY

MRS. MOSS-COCKLE

LONDON
KEGAN PAUL, TRENCH & CO., 1, PATERNOSTER SQUARE
1886

CONTENTS.

Follow Me

Haidée

A Song of England

The Ocean's Prize

In the Sunshine

The Child's Letter

A Hymn ...

Lovely in Death

The Days of Long Ago ...

Willie

The Death of the Old Year ...

Changeless Still

The Little Street-sweeper

Gone Before ...

FOLLOW ME.

"And He said to them all, If any man will come after Me, let him deny himself, and take up his cross daily, and follow Me."
—St. Luke ix. 23.

(*Christ.*)

"Brother, arise, and follow Me,
'Tis I, the Lord, who call to thee,
From wrath to come, and danger flee.
　　Come now, come one and all.
Take up thy cross, and by My might,
Its burden shall be deem'd but light;
For thou must bear it in My sight,
　　Till I shall bid it fall."

"Then when, this weary journey o'er,
Thy feet shall press the golden floor,
Beyond the Jordan's silent shore,
　　That cross will vanish quite.

And on thy brow a crown shall shine,
Whose dazzling lustres will combine
To stamp thee altogether Mine,
    Most precious in My sight."

(1st *Voice in Response.*)

"Yea, Lord, I hear Thee calling me.
From wrath to come I trembling flee,
And Thine I would for ever be,
    But—— "

(*Christ.*)

"But what?"

(*Voice.*)

"The world, it is so wond'rous kind,
My pleasures in it are enshrin'd,
It loves me, and my roving mind
    For God is not yet won.
I am too young to follow Thee,
And give up all so dear to me,
A Christian now I cannot be,
    I'll follow later on!"

(*Christ.*)

"Oh child, so altogether blind,
The world to thee is only kind,
    Because thou 'rt young and fair!
Life's spring-time soon will pass away,
Swift fading into grim decay,
    And Time its joys impair.
Too old and worn to serve Me then,
I ask thy best days now, e'en when
    The flow'r is in its bloom."

(*2nd Voice.*)

"Oh yes! dear Lord, I'll follow Thee,
A Christian ever I would be,
And count all earth as dross to me,
    But———"

(*Christ.*)

    "But what?"

(*Voice.*)

"I am so rich in golden ore,
Houses and lands, a goodly store,
Increasing it still more and more,
    Takes all my thoughts and time.

If I were poor, without this bait
To chain me to my worldly state,
I'd come, and ere it be too late,
    Accept Thy gift divine."

(Christ.)

"Oh brother, my heart bleeds to think
Such trifles stay thee on the brink
    Of endless bliss or woe.
Thy soul I may require of thee,
Before thy goods increas'd shall be;
    With thee they cannot go.
Will they repay thee at that hour,
When death shall hold thee in his pow'r,
    For all thou wilt have lost?"

(3rd Voice.)

"Dear Lord, I hear Thee calling me,
Thy servant should be strong and free,
And I would ever follow Thee,
    But——"

(Christ.)

    "But what?"

(*Voice.*)
"I am so full of household cares,
And daily toils come unawares,
They seem so many traps and snares,
    To banish love divine.
Rarely at rest, I work away,
Fresh cares succeeding day by day,
These are the things, dear Lord, that stay
    My heart from being Thine."

(*Christ.*)
"Oh know, that in thy daily life,
Whether as sister, daughter, wife,
    Thou mayst do work for Me;
Let all thine actions ever prove
The motive principle of love,
    No nobler aim could be.
A household cross to thee is giv'n,
To bear upon thy path to Heav'n,
    So humbly follow Me."

(4*th Voice.*)
"Yes, Lord, I hear Thee calling me,
A better life I long to see—
The world has nearly wearied me,
    But——"

(*Christ.*)

"But what?"

(*Voice.*)

"Foremost in folly's band alway,
I have been gayest of the gay,
What would my friends in wonder say,
    Were I from them to flee?
Alas, my cheeks would burn with shame
To hear them scoffing o'er my name—
Deriding laugh, and jeer, and blame
    My transferr'd love to Thee."

(*Christ.*)

"Oh brother, when thine end draws nigh,
And God decrees that thou must die,
    Will friends avail thee, say?
Can they avert the touch of death,
Or stay the ebbing, flutt'ring breath,
    That soon must cease for aye?
I truly then alone can be,
A friend, a comforter to thee,
    When God calls thee away."

(5*th Voice.*)

"Oh Lord, 'tis true that I would be
A faithful follower of Thee,
From wrath to come I wish to flee,
    But——"

(*Christ.*)

"But what?"

(*Voice.*)

"The dearest one on earth to me,
Perhaps, may never follow Thee,
Apart from him I could not be,
    His love is my true home.
At present he is wilful, blind,
But if, perchance, he change his mind,
And in Thee resting, pure joys find,
    No longer I will roam."

(*Christ.*)

"And canst thou desecrate that love
Which I have given thee to move
    His dark relentless mind?

A woman's influence used aright,
Is stronger than a sword of might,
   With sheath of flowers entwin'd !
Come first, and show him that your heart
Has chosen well that better part,
   He then will follow too."

(*6th Voice.*)

"With much delight I'd follow Thee,
A faithful servant I would be,
These fleeting joys are nought to me,
   But—— "

(*Christ.*)
" But what ? "

(*Voice.*)

"Too old, and weak, and worn am I,
So soon 'twill be that I must die,
I could not follow Thee on high,
   If cross-borne it must be.
As years by decades add their tenth,
They tell me I must sink at length,
Nay, Lord, I have not now the strength
   To humbly follow Thee."

(*Christ.*)

"Oh aged one, in faith so weak,
Thou dost in Me no sweet balm seek,
   To gladden thy last day.
Thank God, before death comes to thee,
That I have call'd thee now to Me,
   Nor cast this chance away;
Delays are dang'rous; all is lost,
  When wav'ring minds by doubts are toss'd,
   And will not, when they may:
For others seize with eager eyes.
The golden gem-besprinkled prize,
   And then they learn, too late,
How much is lost in what has gone,
Which, but for doubts, they might have won.
   So sorrow is their fate!
Both old and young, both grave and gay,
I call to follow Me to-day—
   None are denied My love.
All those who bear a cross for Me
Shall one day radiant ever be,
   With perfect joys in store;
And each one to My side they win,
Rare jewels for their crowns within
   Shall gleam for evermore.

Bright as the glitt'ring stars above,
They'll dwell 'mid heav'nly spheres of love,
   In bliss beyond explore.
Eye hath not seen, nor ear hath heard,
What God hath lovingly conferr'd
   On all who follow Me."

HAIDÉE.

'Twas in the balmy days of June,
When ev'ry hour was fair as noon,
He came—but ah! he came too soon
    To woo her.

And she was debonnaire as May,
Younger than e'en a fresh Spring day,
And sweet as fragrant new-mown hay
    Was Haidée.

The silken ringlets of her hair
Brighter than gold of Ophir were.
They made an aureole so fair
    Around her.

Glow'd in her cheeks the tender blush,
Warm and soft as the morn's first flush,
Quiv'ring all the leaves with a brush
    Fast fleeting.

While in the dewy hazel eyes,
There shone a glimmer of the skies,
Lit by a love that never dies,
    So holy!

Now Ronald, he came from afar,
With honors receiv'd in the war;
So then, when he saw this fair star,
    He lov'd her.

'Twas thus in roseate bowers,
Amidst the odour of flowers,
With dewdrops falling in showers
    He woo'd her.

With the moon's wan light from above,
Smiling down on his own fair dove,
He whisper'd, he whisper'd his love
    To Haidée.

But startled was she as a fawn
That tremblingly bounds o'er the lawn
In the absence of note to warn
    From danger.

Then soothing, he stood by her side,
Crying, "Promise to be my bride."
But her eyes only open'd wide
    With wonder.

Said she, "If 'tis true, all you pray,
Alas! you must go far away,
For to you I never can say
    I love you."

"The one whom I love, he is dead,
Beneath the green sod is his bed;
My love nevermore can be wed
    To mortal."

Quoth Ronald, "Refuse not my flower;
Believe me, you'd have a rich dower,
For with all my soul, and my power,
    I love you."

"But if you say 'nay,' I will die
By these hands, then ever to lie
The victim for years to roll by,
    Of my love."

Spake Haidée, " I give not my love,
But my hand I give thee, to prove
Thy life I would blight not, nor move
    Thee to sin."

The nightingale sang overhead
From the curtain of night outspread;
As the tears of the moon were shed
    In silence.

Oh bright then was that summer time,
Alive with woodbine and the lime,
While soft-eyed blue-bells' muffled chime
    Rang blithely.

Old Time—he flies on airy wings—
O'er them his fairy mantle flings,
And each day passing nearer brings
    Their nuptials.

But 'twas scarce three days off the day
Of the sweet-swelling bridal lay,
That Haidée seem'd to fade away
    In languor.

She faded as the lilies fade,
So quietly, within the shade;
And none could tell whate'er had made
    Her thus die.

'Twas thought she pined away for one
Who to the land of dreams had gone,
But whose fond heart with her's was one
    For ever.

And on the day she should have giv'n
The hand that from her heart was riv'n,
An angel bore her up to Heav'n,—
    To her love.

Thus borne was she from Ronald's side,
Oh nevermore with him to bide;
Stern Death had claim'd her for his bride.
    Fair Haidée!

And Ronald's heart it nearly broke;
Across the sea, he tried to choke
The feelings that could find no cloak
    For sorrow.

In after years he often said,
" I go to where my Haidée sped,
To those pure realms just overhead,
    In Heaven."

A SONG OF ENGLAND.

Oh why is England prosperous,
    And why her people's fare
So free from darksome hopelessness
    And heavy hanging care?
Her strongholds are well fortified,
    Her puissance rules the wave,
And all the hearts of Englishmen
    Are noble, strong, and brave.

Fair plenty decks her star-lit brow
    With crown of inwrought gold,
Her smiles display unsparingly
    Rich mines of wealth untold.
Success her hopes rose-hued doth wreathe,
    And Bounty's outstretch'd hands
Are fill'd for her with riches rare,
    That dower not other lands.

Then why is England prosperous?
    It is because she holds
Religion as her banner true,
    While Virtue it unfolds.
The blessings of the Mighty One
    Descend on England's head,
And bless'd are these her living sons,
    And bless'd her hallow'd dead!

THE OCEAN'S PRIZE.

Onward ever dark waves bore him,
    O'er the surging ocean's foam—
There, where no fond eyes might view him
    In the blue depth's hidden home.
On and on, the wild waves crashing,
    Crushing him in their embrace,
All their dolorous dirges ringing
    O'er the deathful, dappl'd space.

Yes, a dreamy downy pillow
    Did to him the weird waves prove,
Rock'd on briny, bristling billows,
    He was borne from life and love;

Yes, alas! from hearts that lov'd him,
    Friends to whom he was most dear,
Close those seething surges shrin'd him—
    Coffin'd in their yawning bier.

Pale and firm, the mute mouth wearing
    Still a soften'd, pensive smile—
And the sad eyes, half-clos'd, bearing
    Tears for those he lov'd awhile.
Masses of lank hair lay dripping
    O'er that pure brow, marble-white,
E'er in waves of froth deep dipping,
    Shining in the dying light.

Ah! what sighs and prayers were flowing
    Soulful agonies of grief,
For the one on billows tossing,
    Gather'd now in Death's pale sheaf.
He was to his wife, her dearest,
    To his children, all in all,
Once their pride, their star, their glory,
    Now he's far beyond recall.

Stately plumes no sighs were waving,
    From church-bells no groans were rung,

THE OCEAN'S PRIZE.

For the form the waves were laving,
    Never requiem was sung.
But o'ershadowing spirits shining,
    Made a halo o'er the sea,
Closely clasp'd their arms about him,
    Wing'd him to eternity.

IN THE SUNSHINE.

(This song is set to music by C. W. Thomas, Esq., and published by Hart & Co.)

In the sunshine, when the flowers
    Fill the air with perfum'd love,
And the silv'ry clouds are sailing
    In their sapphire seas above;
When the world with smiles is beaming,
    Steeped in languors fair to see,
Will you then remember, darling,
    All you promis'd me to be—
On the day when, crowned with roses,
    Standing in your golden May,
You allur'd with softest glances
    All the heart I had away?

Phantom weird, and worn, and weary,
    Ghastly, grim, and stern, defies
All the sobbing of my being,
    All the tear-drops of my eyes.
Nevermore within the sunshine,
    Down the jewell'd path of flow'rs,
Shall I wander with you, darling,
    'Neath those rose-entwining bow'rs.
When our heart's fond love combining,
    With this world no more shall be,
Then you will become, my darling,
    All you promis'd me to be.

THE CHILD'S LETTER.

"Oh Cissy is so ill, mamma,
   She looks so thin and wan,
The light has left her dancing eyes,
   The rosy hue is gone;
She lies serenely still in bed,
   Nor stirs her head to see
Her Robin gazing for the smile
   He loves so tenderly.

"Say, will she die, my dear mamma?
   I think my heart would break,
If nevermore with me again,
   Her woodland walks she'll take.

The doctor, can't he make her well?
    He cured our little Jane;
So write to him at once to come
    And see her yet again."

The mother wrote, then gently turn'd
    Her weary, woe-worn eyes,
With uprais'd finger, solemnly
    Towards the clear blue skies.
" 'Tis only One, who reigns above,
    Can make her well and strong;
Ask God to spare her precious life—
    To Him all lives belong."

The child look'd grave, and ran away
    On some idea intent,
The one thought uppermost, that nigh
    His heaving bosom rent.
" If mamma can write to doctor,
    To God then, I can write,
Oh where is a pen and paper?
    I'll write this very night."

" Dear God," he wrote, "please will you make
    My little sister well?"

Then he clos'd it, and address'd it,
    But how—I cannot tell;
Nor did he e'en forget to put
    A stamp where it should be,
While to the pillar-box he flew,
    And posted it with glee.

"Oh when will God write back?" he mus'd,
    So proudly pleas'd he seem'd,
For, full of faith and confidence,
    His starry dark eyes gleam'd.
And to mamma, all smiles, he went,
    To tell what he had done;
Then she bent tenderly, and kiss'd
    Her little angel-son.

"God won't write back, dear child," she said,
    "If 'tis His will to give
What you desire, oh then, be sure,
    Our Cissy, she will live.
His will be done! So come with me,
    May be her sleep is o'er."
And softly did they enter through
    The thickly muffled door.

Slowly the clos'd eyes open'd now,
　　With calm inquiring gaze,
To the dear faces bending low
　　Their lambent love-lit rays.
The fever had abated, so
　　The crisis thus was o'er :
"God *has* receiv'd my letter then,"
　　Said Robin ; nothing more.

A HYMN.

Oh come in the rosy morning,
    When new life and hope are strong,
And the heart is beating bravely
    For a conflict fierce and long.
And clad in Christian armour,
    With Faith's banner floating free,
Never the strength shall flicker,
    Till life's battles cease to be.

Oh come in the golden noontide,
    When the heart is bow'd with care,
When the pain and pleasure, mingled,
    Are heavy and hard to bear.

When perfume divine from Heaven,
    Like dew on a thirsty leaf,
Shall be as the balm of Gilead,
    A perfect and sweet relief.

Oh come in the dusky twilight,
    When the strength is almost flown,
And the sear'd heart's fragrant roses
    Are wither'd, and crush'd, and blown.
And a beacon star of glory
    Shall lighten the cloudy way,
To where fadeless flow'rs are blooming,
    In spheres of undying day.

Oh come in the silent midnight,
    When life's journey is nearly o'er,
And the soul is only waiting
    To pass to the far-off shore.
When with love unknown, unbounded,
    The unseen Christ shall guide
Over the waters of Jordan,
    Safe, safe to the other side.

LOVELY IN DEATH.

Thou fair young form of maidenhood;
   Making e'en death a lovely sight,
Just in the flush of life's sweet bloom,
   How soon thy day is turn'd to night.

The absence of the vital spark
   Disrobes thy features of no charm,
Rather, the impress it has left
   Has serv'd to paint them bright and warm.

Thy hair wears still its glossy hue,
   Twining and twisting o'er thy brow,
As if 'twould scoff the hand of death,
   And mock its presence even now.

Lovely those eyes, so large, so deep,
    Breathing a love, in sooth, divine,
Bright with the ray thy spirit left,
    In Heav'n's own halo do they shine.

Those veiling lashes, curl'd and dark,
    Contrast well with thy marble cheek :
The chisell'd nose—the clear-cut lips—
    Make all description poor and weak.

Thy dress so white, the rose that lies
    Upon thy stirless silent breast,
Are emblems of the hidden life
    Thy soul has found in endless rest.

Thou casket of a deathless gem,
    Now in the grave at peace shall lie,
Till the last trump of God shall sound
    To bid thee join thy soul on high !

THE DAYS OF LONG AGO.

(This song is set to music by C. W. Thomas, Esq., and published by Hart & Co.)

By the riverside they wander'd,
    In the days of long ago,
When their youthful hearts were throbbing
    With a passion-piercing glow;
When the star-strown smiling future
    Lit the fervour of their love
Into a spark as radiant
    As undying flames above.
"For ever mine"—"For ever thine"—
    Ah! well their troth they spoke,
While the pale sun gleam'd above them,
    And the silver wavelets broke.

'Twas but a living dream,
   Now, at length, they know,
For nevermore returning
   Are the days of long ago!

'Neath an aspen's quiv'ring branches,
   By a green and mossy mound,
Shrouded in a veil of sorrow,
   So an aged man is found.
Hoary, bent, convuls'd with sorrow,
   For the love of long ago,
Does his soul discharge its anguish,
   As but truest love can flow.
By the riverside no longer
   Will they wander as of yore,
For the golden light of morning
   O'er their hearts can break no more.
'Twas but a living dream,
   Now, at length, they know,
For nevermore returning
   Are the days of long ago!

WILLIE.

I took his tiny hand in mine,
    I kiss'd his fevered cheek,
Pressing the frail form in my arms,
    The form that was so weak.

I rain'd bright tear-drops on the head
    That shone with golden hair,
Gazing into the deep blue eyes,
    The face that was so fair.

I knew the blossom in my arms
    Was fading fast away,
That ere the morn 'twould garner'd be,
    To bloom in deathless day.

And strangely did my pulses throb,
　　And anguish pierc'd my heart,
That I must from the child I lov'd,
　　So soon, so sadly part.

But messengers from fairer spheres
　　A Father's summons bore;
So how should I, though left behind,
　　His happiness deplore?

And then a low voice smote my ear,
　　I heard my darling say,
" I'm going, going far from you,
　　With you I cannot stay."

" I've lov'd to play in ilex groves,
　　Chasing the butterfly,
But now my Father bids me rise
　　To fairer bowers on high."

" And, think you, God will let me cull
　　Flow'rs for a garland gay,
And play in streets all pav'd with gold,
　　Throughout the livelong day?"

" I do not weep to leave you here,
 For I shall watch on high,
To be the first to welcome you
 To mansions in the sky."

" I only ask the flow'rs I love
 May lie upon my breast,
When, having bid farewell to all,
 You lay me down to rest !"

Alas, I heard no more from him,
 The pretty golden head
Sank gently, slowly down again
 Upon the snowy bed.

I saw the blue eyes rais'd on high
 To those pure realms above ;
And then I felt him borne away
 On angel-wings of love.

Then did I cut a silken curl
 That rested on my arm,
Whispering softly to myself,
 " My Willie's safe from harm."

Yes, pillowed on a Father's breast,
    And in a Father's home,
He'll henceforth know nor sin nor pain,
    And sorrow ne'ermore come.

Of him I never cease to think,
    Nor do I e'er forget
To strew my Willie's grave with flow'rs—
    The rose, and violet.

THE DEATH OF THE OLD YEAR.

I can hear the church-bells ringing
    O'er the jewel-sprinkl'd snow,
As the dying light of sunset
    Flames the heavens all aglow.
And the glaciers, stiffly hanging
    From the leafless arms on high,
Shine as diamonds gleaming brightly
    In the star-lamps of the sky.

Ruddy red the old log burning,
    Crackles in the rich man's grate,
As the timepiece, beating slowly,
    Tells the hour is growing late.
Old year! hoary with the snow-flakes
    Scatter'd in thy tangled hair,
All prepared to leave thy kingdom
    To the baby small and fair.

Give a blessing, ere thou takest
    All the old and lov'd hours spent,
That the joy of having liv'd them
    May with mem'ry sweet be blent;
So into the untrod regions
    Of the future's unknown ways,
Perfect light may guide us rightly,
    Lit with true-love's quenchless rays.

CHANGELESS STILL.

(This song is set to music by C. W. Thomas, Esq., and published by Hart & Co.)

In the dawning, when the sunlight
   Stream'd upon the sleepy flow'rs,
And the wind was shaking gently
   Show'rs of dew from off the bow'rs,—
Came a maiden tripping softly,
   With the love-light in her eyes,
To the trysting-tree where, waiting,
   Her belovèd she espies.
"Can you love me thus, and leave me?"
   Cried she in that parting hour;—
And his word, "For ever changeless,"
   Held her in its soothing pow'r.

CHANGELESS STILL.

In the dawning, after years,
  Years of waiting and regret,
Came the maiden stepping sadly,
  While her eyes with tears are wet.
'Neath the trysting-tree she gazes,—
  Stands an angel waiting there!
Can it be her heart's belovèd,
  Come from realms divinely fair?
"Changeless still," he murmur'd softly,
  "Death is not so strong as love,
And I've come to fetch you, darling,
  To a better world above."

THE LITTLE STREET-SWEEPER.

Poor little fellow ! cold and thin,
    Brushing with all his might,
He sees not the shadows gath'ring
    In the dark drizzling night.

The lamps are lit, and radiate
    His worn and weary face,
Great eyes down-dropt, and features too—
    Possessing winning grace.

"Give me a penny, please," he cries.
    With pleading tones and sad ;
The people merely hurry on,
    Nor heed the little lad.

He gazes listly after them,
   The blue eyes dim with tears;
Long sobs break from his heaving breast,
   His heart beats fast with fears.

"Nothing to eat; nowhere to sleep!"
   Oh, that the rich would turn
From their cruel scorn to hear him,
   Before his case they spurn.

A fearful lack of sympathy,
   A woeful want of heart;
Ah! who can be a Christian,
   And take no Christian's part?

Ye who refuse a pittance to
   The smallest, ay, of those
Who ask it — then remember that
   God marks it, and He knows.

"As much as ye did not do it
   To those who needy be,
So I count it that ye did not
   Thus do it unto Me."

GONE BEFORE.

Oh give me back the golden years,
   Of the time when, long ago,
Sweet sun-kist smiles did woo the hours,
   And a tear we ne'er did know.
When flow'r-hung joys, bestrewn with gems,
   Drops ambrosial shed around;
And the gentle forms of dear ones,
   Loving arms around us wound.

They, too, have pass'd to join the throng,
   Round the mystic great white throne,
While their vacant places leave us,
   Ah, so weary, sad, and lone.
Only echoes of their voices
   Steal along the evening air--
As we dream we see them sitting
   By our side, as once they were.

Angels, whisp'ring in the silence
    Of the hush'd and starry night,
Waft the deathless germs to usward,
    From their fire-tipp'd wings of light.
And they sprout as trees, life-giving—
    Fruit, that ne'er can wither more,
Ready ripen'd to be garner'd
    In the vast eternal store.

MATTIE IN THE CLOISTERS.

WEARILY a little figure,
    Barely clad, and thin, and ill,
Sought the shelter of the cloisters—
    Where, beneath the arches still,
Found he solace from the sorrow
    Of an outside world of care,
That made life, in years so tender,
    Sad and clouded, sear'd and bare.

Grandly through the vaulted arches
    Stole the organ's richest tones,
Swelling into soulful volumes,
    Dying into murm'ring moans.

Striking sore poor Mattie's heartstrings,
  While the big tears dimm'd his eyes,
Till the sobs that struggling shook him
  Brought an angel from the skies.

Slowly down the aisle appearing,
  Came she robed in sheen of white,
And her face was fair and beaming
  With a sweet unearthly light.
Mattie wonder'd at the vision,
  Like a child, no fear arose,
And he seem'd as though admiring
  The strange beauty of her clothes.

Very tenderly she kiss'd him,
  Then she bore him far away,
Past the scenes where he in gladness
  Oft did with his comrades play.
Over hedge, and tree, and flower,
  To the golden cloudless land,
Where the children meet together
  Playing on its shining strand.

Back the gates of pearl and jacinth,
  And the lady enter'd in;

But without did little Mattie
    Leave his soil-stain'd shroud of sin.
With the robe of Christ his Saviour,
    Far from want, and scorn, and pain,
Never will he seek for shelter
    In an earthly court again.

LOVE IN THE GLADE.

Love went stalking in the glade,
    With a lightsome bounding heart,
Holding in his golden sheath
    Many a bright bejewell'd dart.
Looking near, and gazing far,
    Pluming oft his wings of light,
Now he sees a maiden fair,
    Rob'd in virgin garb of white;
Sad she seems—she has no love
    To give life unto her life;
So he pulls his silken string,
    And he asks her for his wife.
Love is sadness, love is gladness,
Love sometimes is only madness!

LOVE IN THE GLADE.

Love went sighing in the shade,
   In the waning of the day,
But one arrow in his hand,—
   All the rest were cast away;
They had pierc'd so many hearts,
   Wringing drops of ruddy gore,
That, grown weary of his play,
   He resolv'd to shoot no more.
Regretful of the plunder
   That made havoc of his life,
He fell amongst the flowers,
   On his own red reeking knife.
Love is sadness, love is gladness,
Love sometimes is only madness!

A MAY BRIDAL.

SHE stood in clouds of snowy white,
My bride, the darling of my sight,
Her soft eyes gleaming with a light
    Of deepest joy.

The raven tresses of her hair
Hung down in masses rich and rare,
Clustering o'er a brow as fair
    As lilies are.

Her long silk lashes, dew'd with tears,
Reveal'd the heart of many fears;
She seem'd a rose that conscious rears
    To heav'n its head.

A thousand blushes came and went,
As she her fair head lowly bent,
And heart's fond pray'r to God was sent,
    My love—my bride.

The organ roll'd out through the place,
I scarce could see my darling's face—
'Twas hid in shimm'ring sheen of lace
    As she approach'd.

I felt her kneeling by my side,—
The golden knot at last was tied,
For evermore with me to bide,
    Oh, bliss supreme!

The Church rite o'er—to tell the rest—
Of mingl'd greetings, sweet and blest—
I clasp'd her to my loving breast,
    My life, my all.

One year of happiness so bright,
One year of blessing and delight,
Then unto God she wing'd her flight.
    Oh earth! oh love!

I look back on the time gone by,
To soothe my grief I'd fain not try,
My heart is rent—I only sigh
    For death to come.

Oh, that my tongue could ever tell
The love my heart has known so well,
Profound and silent must it dwell
    Till heav'n be mine.

POET AND PHILOSOPHER.

(*Philosopher.*)

I am an orbit, whose keen eye of light
Can pierce through the dawning, and probe the night.

Sheer shams and dumb shows I shiver, and shake
To all the four winds the idols ye make.

The world is an open book in my hand,
In it I read mystic truths of the land.

(*Poet.*)

I am the spirit that filleth all space,
For in earth and heav'n my light is God's face.

The spark I kindle from altars of fire,
Sets the world's soul all aflame with desire.

All men are my subjects, for all hearts are mine ;
The sceptre I wield i' my hand is divine.

(Epilogue.)

Philosophers treat of the things that are,
   A noble mission, as all may see ;
But the poets are God's ambassadors,
   They show alone how those things should be.

A DREAM OF APOLLO.

I sit beside the sedgy stream that runs
   Rippling and rushing by my weary feet;
Above, the birds are singing in the trees,
    And in the distance, sounds the young lamb's bleat.
      So drowsy is the air,
       The parting light paints fair
Many an Iris line of beauty in the sky,
Till it and earth both kiss each other silently.

Athwart the grass, the shadows come and go,
   Playing a fairy gambol in the stream,
As o'er me, while the rushes bend and bow,
    It seems a veil enwraps me—and I dream;
      For through yon wicket gate,
      Where Nora used to wait,

(Ah me! she's singing now beyond the stars of God,)
There comes a gliding figure towards me, o'er the sod.

His eyes are flaming stars, and round his brow
    A wreath of twisted laurel is entwin'd,
His face, dead-pale, reveals the inward fire
    Where, in his soul, immortal thoughts are shrin'd.
        A hero dear to fame,
        In sooth, I know his name,
Apollo come from Arcady! and in his hand
A lyre—that lyre which chains and charms the list-
    'ning land.

He spoke not, though I long'd to hear him speak,
    But silently struck sundry chords that rang
Through all my veins and fibres, thrilling me;
    Then in full flute-like, tender tones, he sang:—

    "When hearts are weary, and love is sad,
        Fond hope from our soul seems flying.
    The flow'rs with a weight of tears are bent,
        And Nature's sweet self seems dying.
        Alas! alas! and well-a-day!
    When hearts are weary, and love is sad.

When joy peeps out from a dove-grey cloud,
   Like the sun, which e'er is shining,
Though dusky hued is the cloud awhile,
   It still has a silver lining.
     Alas! alas! and well-a-day!
When joy peeps out from a dove-grey cloud.

Love is the essence and life of life
   To the heart that's worn and weary,
And sweet content is a lamp that turns
   Into day the night so dreary.
     Alas! alas! and well-a-day!
Love is the essence and life of life."

The lyre is hush'd—through all the trees the wind
   Is echoing the burden of the song;
I gaze and gaze, but lo! he is not there,
   He stands not in the leafy shrubs among.
     The night is drawing near,
     The stars are shining clear,
And as the dew-kist eyelids of the twilight close,
A pent-up truant tear fell silently.   I rose.

A RED ROSE.

'Twas all on a July evening,
   The mellowing summer time—
When the perfume-laden breezes
   To the choir-bird's anthems chime,
That he gave a red, red rose-bud
   To his darling, standing there,
And she placed it in the ripples
   Of her sun-lit, shining hair.
"Plight me your troth on that, dearest,
   Oh plight me your troth to-day."
So she gave him her heart for ever,
   Her love, and her life, for aye.

Far over the blue sea billows
    Her sailor must go to roam;
His love he leaves with his darling,
    Her heart is his only home.
But she pal'd and pin'd as the flow'r
    That wither'd upon her breast;
While Death kiss'd her eyes—to waken
    In realms of eternal rest.
"Still mine, for Heav'n will unite us,"
    Her sailor cried sore that day,
" For do I not know she gave me
    Her love, and her life, for aye?"

THE WOODCUTTER'S DAUGHTER.

A cold wind in the silent night
   Did whistle through the trees,
And borne away was many a leaf
   By the alluring breeze.
The bat's cry echoed through the wood,
   The pale stars shone on high,
Glimmering in a setting dark
   Of amaranthine sky.

One lonely hut was pictur'd there,
   Amid the weird, wan scene;
It seem'd to stare from out the gloom
   With chilly look serene.

THE WOODCUTTER'S DAUGHTER.

A dim light in the casement burnt,
    A window broken through,
And bitterly the midnight wind
    O'er that dark, dank hut blew.

Inside was stretch'd upon a mat
    Old Jeff, the woodcutter,
Who fast in low and mournful tones,
    To himself did mutter.
Writhing upon his narrow bed,
    In dreadful pain he lay,
For ne'er could he again expect
    To see the light of day.

A gentle face look'd sadly down
    Upon the old man there,
All lovely as a blushing rose,
    So sweet, so fresh, so fair.
The soul-lit eyes bedew'd with tears,
    The coral lips compress'd,
As with her pale and trembling hands
    His mortal wound she dress'd.

Not long the old man had to wait
    Heav'n's messenger to come,

Who bore him from his pains and woes,
  To a celestial home.
Or ere the first faint flush of morn
  Burst on his earth-pall'd sight,
His soul was wafted to the realms
  That know no pain or night.

Sweet strains from his dear daughter's voice
  Forthwith to heav'n did ring,
They floated with him as he sped
  Upon the angel's wing.
Alone she stood, that frail, fair form,
  With pallid Death beside ;
Well that he had not claim'd her yet
  For his resistless bride.

But guardian spirits, visionless,
  In countless train drew near,
And tenderly they wip'd away
  The maiden's heart-wrung tear.
" Away," they whisper'd, " far away,
  You soon will follow, too,
To know, beyond those golden gates,
  What hope and joy ne'er knew."

CHRIST OR DIANA.

(SUGGESTED BY MR. E. LONG'S PICTURE, EXHIBITED AT
THE ROYAL ACADEMY.)

FLUSHES a rosy hue aslant the sky,
Aurora smiles; the solemn hour draws nigh
That shall decide the freedom of a life
Chain'd down, and bound, beneath a nation's knife,
Debas'd, and fetter'd to caprice of will,
Oh who but for a gain untold, could bear it still?
Lo, where it listeth, doth the Boreas blow,
But where it resteth, can we never know.
Alike the ray which probes the wounds of night,
Transpierc'd a hopeless blindness into sight;
And o'er the desert of a maiden's heart
Diffus'd such radiance that new life did start,

Now breaking forth, on eagle wings to soar
Where Faith and Sight unite for evermore.
The moment come—the multitude around,
Beneath the tow'ring buildings closely wound,
Rang'd high in tiers, in dappled hues gaze on,
To see which triumph may the day have won.
"Christ or Diana," rings along the sea,
"Let her but cast one grain, and she is free."
Clad in her vestal robe of white she stands;
'Tis hers, by one small act, to burst her bands—
Freedom or bondage choose, yea, heav'n or hell,
The tremour of that moment who can tell?
Reigns now a strange, dead silence—all await
To see a slave dissolve this grain of fate.
Blanch'd with a pallor that reveals the pain,
Her features set, the eyes uprais'd again,
Her soul speaks through them to the eager throng,
Of high resolving, noble, pure and strong;
Of unseen presence felt, whose aid is near,
At this all-trying moment, to o'ercome each fear.
"Avaunt, Diana! Bondage do I brave!"
Is the averting movement of the slave.
"Shall one dire grain possess pow'r to recall
The sentence that a lifetime doth enthrall?

Or buy my soul from Him who died to prove
The deep reality of His great love.
Nay, rather bondage with its hundred years,
Than reeking misery of shame and tears.
Christ ever! though a while in bonds to be,
A Christian's crown shall set the slave-girl free."

A LOVE-PORTRAIT.

The life of love, the light of life shone round,
'Mid cloudless skies, from loving trustful eyes,
Heav'n in their glance, and rapture in each touch,
With joy heart-throbbing, and with tender sighs.

Behold a wife, a mother, 'neath the shade
Of softly brushing leaves and nodding flow'rs,
Her child upon her knee, while for his weal
Her thoughts were busy through the sunny hours.

Sweet smil'd her hero—her belovèd lord,
Reclining on the green grass waving there;
His dark curls, ruffled by the fitful wind,
Display'd a brow as noble as 'twas fair.

And oft the child would wander forth to cull
Some woodland flow'ret in the meadow near,
Returning to his parents, gleeful, wild,
To pour his prating prattle in their ear.

Oh, gentle wife, so worthily ador'd,
And husband, so befitting to be guide,
Walk onwards, hand in hand, while yet 'tis day,
Then rest together in life's eventide.

WOMAN'S RIGHTS.

Women true, and pure, and fair,
With the love-crown in your hair,
Would you men's stern mission share?

Seek you men to emulate?
Claim your votes—and in debate
Model laws of Church and State?

Forsooth, 'tis an aggressive age,
All are as Minerva, sage,
Ready wisdom's war to wage.

Henceforth men no more shall reign—
'Tis the woman's broad domain;
Let them follow in her train.

They must see she holds her own
In contention, and alone
Shareth equally his throne.

Sisters, listen ! it is true
Men have brains, so likewise you,
Yours as good—oft better, too.

But their use should be to shed
Radiant blessings on the head
Of home's dear ones gathered.

So, by firm but loving hand,
Lead a mighty angel-band
Safely to the better land.

Science, Art, will sweeter be,
If in them God's love you see,
Who has given them to thee.

Thus your brain's creations grow,
Swift in broadest paths to flow,
With inspirèd flame aglow.

May your pow'r supreme which sways
Man, whom e'er your will obeys,
Glitter in life's love-strung rays.

That your influence may shine,
And as ivy-leaves entwine
Round the world, and home—divine.

TRIFLES MAKE THE SUM OF LIFE.

Oh is there not a sweetness in the smallest flow'r
    that grows,
The dewdrop on the green leaf, the zephyr wind that
    blows,
The broad fields, and the wild flow'rs that bestrew the
    path we tread,
The odours of the roses, and the songsters overhead?

And our God has not forgotten the smallest things
    that please,
The brooklet's faintest murmurs, or the music on the
    breeze;
Though power and majesty are His beyond this world's
    compare,
The tiny flow'rs are sweetest, and the children are His
    care.

The daily round of duty, the daily task of love,
Howe'er trifling, savours of the angels' work above.
The gentle smile in passing, the kind word on the way—
Germs oft in richest blossom to bloom in cloudless day.

The love that speaks in silent acts, the true devoted heart,
Can never give enough of joy, enough of good impart;
But love is not a trifle—nor should we deem it so,
It is our hope, our joy, our trust, our bane, our weal, or woe.

Yes, little kindly actions far more than words do tell,
What clear and plainest language could never say so well.
Such little loving actions, done by tender, gentle hands,
Will leave their marks indelible on life's own golden sands.

Oh, life's made up of trifles, as of drops the ocean blue,
They waft us to Eternity—that path all must pursue.

Then let us ne'er waste a minute, of those that God has giv'n,
Since each one passing nears us to the pearly gates of heav'n.

KING CYRUS' CAPTIVES.

Before the presence of august King Cyrus,
    In all the glory of his regal sway,
A heathen Prince, wife, children, household, captives,
    Came, 'neath their galling yoke of fears, that day.

A voiceless misery of mute pain, dumb woe,
    That Prince's eyes reveal'd, still more his gait ;
Bent by the blasting blow of bondage, surely
    Grim death were sweeter than this sterner state.

The King spake gently—with a pitying eye
    On one so young, so noble, and so sad—
"Say, what wilt thou give thy children to redeem?"
    He answer'd, "All, all in the world he had."

"But giving all for them, what yet remainest,
   What ransom canst thou offer for thy wife?"
The captive spoke in clear, unfaltering tones,
   "For her I'll forfeit, sire, my very life."

"Freedom to you and yours," rejoin'd King Cyrus.
   "Begone—I spare your dear ones, and your life."
They left that mighty presence—and the air was
   With his praises, and their thankful cries, all rife.

So home they journey'd, descanting as they went
   On Persia's monarch, and his noble heart,
But one tongue was silent, though the thoughts ran deep;
   One only in his praises bore no part.

What seem'd ungracious the Prince's ire arous'd,
   Who straightway ask'd his wife why this should be?
"I can but think of one," in tears she answer'd,
   "Of one who would his life have giv'n for me."

If, like this captive's wife, our hearts and hopes
   Were centred in that Love which died to free
Us from a direr bondage than earth's fetters,
   Our lives by such sweet thoughts would nobler be.

AQUA VITÆ.

Through the little lives of men
Flows a stream, by rock and glen,
Clear or turbid, now and then.

Sometimes fring'd with nodding flow'rs,
Jewell'd by the shining show'rs,
Hanging o'er lone lazy bow'rs.

Oftener twin'd in tangled weed,
Long-lash'd marsh, and rank-grown reed,
In the gloom beneath the mead.

Runs the current never still—
Foaming, gurgling down the hill
To some far and unknown rill.

Flowers of pleasure by that stream,
Gliding in yon glancing gleam,
Life is not one golden dream.

Drifting stream! we ne'er can know
How you glide, nor where you go,
But through all our veins you flow.

And your path for aye must run,
Through the shade, and through the sun,
Till its course be duly done.

Then to join the Jasper sea,
Where the blue waves smilingly
Roll into Eternity.

THE END.

A LIST OF
KEGAN PAUL, TRENCH & CO.'S PUBLICATIONS.

A LIST OF KEGAN PAUL, TRENCH & CO.'S PUBLICATIONS.

CONTENTS.

	PAGE		PAGE
GENERAL LITERATURE.	2	MILITARY WORKS.	33
PARCHMENT LIBRARY	18	POETRY.	34
PULPIT COMMENTARY	20	NOVELS AND TALES	39
INTERNATIONAL SCIENTIFIC SERIES	29	BOOKS FOR THE YOUNG	41

GENERAL LITERATURE.

AINSWORTH, W. F.—A Personal Narrative of the Euphrates Expedition. With Map. 2 vols. Demy 8vo, 30s.

A. K. H. B.—From a Quiet Place. A Volume of Sermons. Crown 8vo, 5s.

ALEXANDER, William, D.D., Bishop of Derry.—The Great Question, and other Sermons. Crown 8vo, 6s.

ALLIES, T. W., M.A.—Per Crucem ad Lucem. The Result of a Life. 2 vols. Demy 8vo, 25s.

A Life's Decision. Crown 8vo, 7s. 6d.

AMHERST, Rev. W. J.—The History of Catholic Emancipation and the Progress of the Catholic Church in the British Isles (chiefly in England) from 1771-1820. 2 vols. Demy 8vo, 24s.

AMOS, Professor Sheldon.—The History and Principles of the Civil Law of Rome. An aid to the Study of Scientific and Comparative Jurisprudence. Demy 8vo, 16s.

Ancient and Modern Britons. A Retrospect. 2 vols. Demy 8vo, 24s.

Are Foreign Missions doing any Good? An Enquiry into their Social Effects. Crown 8vo, 1s.

ARISTOTLE.—**The Nicomachean Ethics of Aristotle.** Translated by F. H. Peters, M.A. Third Edition. Crown 8vo, 6s.

AUBERTIN, J. J.—**A Flight to Mexico.** With 7 full-page Illustrations and a Railway Map of Mexico. Crown 8vo, 7s. 6d.

    Six Months in Cape Colony and Natal. With Illustrations and Map. Crown 8vo, 6s.

    A Fight with Distances. Illustrations and Maps. Crown 8vo, 7s. 6d.

Aucassin and Nicolette. Edited in Old French and rendered in Modern English by F. W. BOURDILLON. Fcap 8vo, 7s. 6d.

AZARIAS, Brother.—**Aristotle and the Christian Church.** Small crown 8vo, 3s. 6d.

BADGER, George Percy, D.C.L.—**An English-Arabic Lexicon.** In which the equivalent for English Words and Idiomatic Sentences are rendered into literary and colloquial Arabic. Royal 4to, 80s.

BAGEHOT, Walter.—**The English Constitution.** Fourth Edition. Crown 8vo, 7s. 6d.

    Lombard Street. A Description of the Money Market. Eighth Edition. Crown 8vo, 7s. 6d.

    Essays on Parliamentary Reform. Crown 8vo, 5s.

    Some Articles on the Depreciation of Silver, and Topics connected with it. Demy 8vo, 5s.

BAGOT, Alan, C.E.—**Accidents in Mines:** their Causes and Prevention. Crown 8vo, 6s.

    The Principles of Colliery Ventilation. Second Edition, greatly enlarged. Crown 8vo, 5s.

    The Principles of Civil Engineering as applied to Agriculture and Estate Management. Crown 8vo, 7s. 6d.

BALDWIN, Capt. J. H.—**The Large and Small Game of Bengal and the North-Western Provinces of India.** With 20 Illustrations. New and Cheaper Edition. Small 4to, 10s. 6d.

BALL, John, F.R.S.—**Notes of a Naturalist in South America.** With Map. Crown 8vo, 8s. 6d.

BALLIN, Ada S. and F. L.—**A Hebrew Grammar.** With Exercises selected from the Bible. Crown 8vo, 7s. 6d.

BASU, K. P., M.A.—**Students' Mathematical Companion.** Containing problems in Arithmetic, Algebra, Geometry, and Mensuration, for Students of the Indian Universities. Crown 8vo, 6s.

BAUR, *Ferdinand, Dr. Ph.*—A Philological Introduction to Greek and Latin for Students. Translated and adapted from the German, by C. KEGAN PAUL, M.A., and E. D. STONE, M.A. Third Edition. Crown 8vo, 6s.

BAYLY, *Capt. George.*—Sea Life Sixty Years Ago. A Record of Adventures which led up to the Discovery of the Relics of the long-missing Expedition commanded by the Comte de la Perouse. Crown 8vo, 3s. 6d.

BENSON, *A. C.*—William Laud, sometime Archbishop of Canterbury. A Study. With Portrait. Crown 8vo, 6s.

BLACKBURN, *Mrs. Hugh.*—Bible Beasts and Birds. 22 Illustrations of Scripture photographed from the Original. 4to, 42s.

BLOOMFIELD, *The Lady.*—Reminiscences of Court and Diplomatic Life. New and Cheaper Edition. With Frontispiece. Crown 8vo, 6s.

BLUNT, *The Ven. Archdeacon.*—The Divine Patriot, and other Sermons. Preached in Scarborough and in Cannes. New and Cheaper Edition. Crown 8vo, 4s. 6d.

BLUNT, *Wilfrid S.*—The Future of Islam. Crown 8vo, 6s.

Ideas about India. Crown 8vo. Cloth, 6s.

BOWEN, *H. C., M.A.*—Studies in English. For the use of Modern Schools. Ninth Thousand. Small crown 8vo, 1s. 6d.

English Grammar for Beginners. Fcap. 8vo, 1s.

Simple English Poems. English Literature for Junior Classes. In four parts. Parts I., II., and III., 6d. each. Part IV., 1s. Complete, 3s.

BRADLEY, *F. H.*—The Principles of Logic. Demy 8vo, 16s.

BRIDGETT, *Rev. T. E.*—History of the Holy Eucharist in Great Britain. 2 vols. Demy 8vo, 18s.

BROOKE, *Rev. Stopford A.*—The Fight of Faith. Sermons preached on various occasions. Fifth Edition. Crown 8vo, 7s. 6d.

The Spirit of the Christian Life. Third Edition. Crown 8vo, 5s.

Theology in the English Poets.—Cowper, Coleridge, Wordsworth, and Burns. Sixth Edition. Post 8vo, 5s.

Christ in Modern Life. Sixteenth Edition. Crown 8vo, 5s.

Sermons. First Series. Thirteenth Edition. Crown 8vo, 5s.

Sermons. Second Series. Sixth Edition. Crown 8vo, 5s.

BROWN, *Horatio F.*—Life on the Lagoons. With 2 Illustrations and Map. Crown 8vo, 6s.

Venetian Studies. Crown 8vo, 7s. 6d.

BROWN, *Rev. J. Baldwin.*—The Higher Life. Its Reality, Experience, and Destiny. Sixth Edition. Crown 8vo, 5s.

    Doctrine of Annihilation in the Light of the Gospel of Love. Five Discourses. Fourth Edition. Crown 8vo, 2s. 6d.

    The Christian Policy of Life. A Book for Young Men of Business. Third Edition. Crown 8vo, 3s. 6d.

BURDETT, *Henry C.*—Help in Sickness—Where to Go and What to Do. Crown 8vo, 1s. 6d.

    Helps to Health. The Habitation—The Nursery—The Schoolroom and—The Person. With a Chapter on Pleasure and Health Resorts. Crown 8vo, 1s. 6d.

BURKE, *Oliver J.*—South Isles of Aran (County Galway). Crown 8vo, 2s. 6d.

BURKE, *The Late Very Rev. T. N.*—His Life. By W. J. FITZPATRICK. 2 vols. With Portrait. Demy 8vo, 30s.

BURTON, *Lady.*—The Inner Life of Syria, Palestine, and the Holy Land. Post 8vo, 6s.

CANDLER, *C.*—The Prevention of Consumption. A Mode of Prevention founded on a New Theory of the Nature of the Tubercle-Bacillus. Demy 8vo, 10s. 6d.

CAPES, *J. M.*—The Church of the Apostles: an Historical Inquiry. Demy 8vo, 9s.

CARPENTER, *W. B.*—The Principles of Mental Physiology. With their Applications to the Training and Discipline of the Mind, and the Study of its Morbid Conditions. Illustrated. Sixth Edition. 8vo, 12s.

    Nature and Man. With a Memorial Sketch by the Rev. J. ESTLIN CARPENTER. Portrait. Large crown 8vo, 8s. 6d.

Catholic Dictionary. Containing some Account of the Doctrine, Discipline, Rites, Ceremonies, Councils, and Religious Orders of the Catholic Church. By WILLIAM E. ADDIS and THOMAS ARNOLD, M.A. Third Edition. Demy 8vo, 21s.

Century Guild Hobby Horse. Vols. I. and II. Half parchment, 12s. 6d. each.

CHARLES, *Rev. R. H.*—Forgiveness, and other Sermons. Crown 8vo, 4s. 6d.

CHEYNE, *Canon.*—The Prophecies of Isaiah. Translated with Critical Notes and Dissertations. 2 vols. Fourth Edition. Demy 8vo, 25s.

    Job and Solomon; or, the Wisdom of the Old Testament. Demy 8vo, 12s. 6d.

    The Psalms; or, Book of The Praises of Israel. Translated with Commentary. Demy 8vo. 16s.

Churgress, The. By "THE PRIG." Fcap. 8vo, 3s. 6d.

CLAIRAUT.—Elements of Geometry. Translated by Dr. KAINES. With 145 Figures. Crown 8vo, 4s. 6d.

CLAPPERTON, Jane Hume.—Scientific Meliorism and the Evolution of Happiness. Large crown 8vo, 8s. 6d.

CLARKE, Rev. Henry James, A.K.C.—The Fundamental Science. Demy 8vo, 10s. 6d.

CLODD, Edward, F.R.A.S.—The Childhood of the World: a Simple Account of Man in Early Times. Eighth Edition. Crown 8vo, 3s.
    A Special Edition for Schools. 1s.

    The Childhood of Religions. Including a Simple Account of the Birth and Growth of Myths and Legends. Eighth Thousand. Crown 8vo, 5s.
    A Special Edition for Schools. 1s. 6d.

    Jesus of Nazareth. With a brief sketch of Jewish History to the Time of His Birth. Small crown 8vo, 6s.

COGHLAN, J. Cole, D.D.—The Modern Pharisee and other Sermons. Edited by the Very Rev. H. H. DICKINSON, D.D., Dean of Chapel Royal, Dublin. New and Cheaper Edition. Crown 8vo, 7s. 6d.

COLERIDGE, Sara.—Memoir and Letters of Sara Coleridge. Edited by her Daughter. With Index. Cheap Edition. With Portrait. 7s. 6d.

COLERIDGE, The Hon. Stephen.—Demetrius. Crown 8vo, 5s.

CONNELL, A. K.—Discontent and Danger in India. Small crown 8vo, 3s. 6d.

    The Economic Revolution of India. Crown 8vo, 4s. 6d.

COOK, Keningale, LL.D.—The Fathers of Jesus. A Study of the Lineage of the Christian Doctrine and Traditions. 2 vols. Demy 8vo, 28s.

CORR, the late Rev. T. J., M.A.—Favilla; Tales, Essays, and Poems. Crown 8vo, 5s.

CORY, William.—A Guide to Modern English History. Part I.—MDCCCXV.-MDCCCXXX. Demy 8vo, 9s. Part II.—MDCCCXXX.-MDCCCXXXV., 15s.

COTTON, H. J. S.—New India, or India in Transition. Third Edition. Crown 8vo, 4s. 6d.; Cheap Edition, paper covers, 1s.

COWIE, Right Rev. W. G.—Our Last Year in New Zealand. 1887. Crown 8vo, 7s. 6d.

COX, Rev. Sir George W., M.A., Bart.—The Mythology of the Aryan Nations. New Edition. Demy 8vo, 16s.

COX, *Rev. Sir George W., M.A., Bart.—continued.*

    Tales of Ancient Greece. New Edition. Small crown 8vo, 6s.

    A Manual of Mythology in the form of Question and Answer. New Edition. Fcap. 8vo, 3s.

    An Introduction to the Science of Comparative Mythology and Folk-Lore. Second Edition. Crown 8vo, 7s. 6d.

COX, *Rev. Sir G. W., M.A., Bart., and* JONES, *Eustace Hinton.*—Popular Romances of the Middle Ages. Third Edition, in 1 vol. Crown 8vo, 6s.

COX, *Rev. Samuel, D.D.*—A Commentary on the Book of Job. With a Translation. Second Edition. Demy 8vo, 15s.

    Salvator Mundi; or, Is Christ the Saviour of all Men? Tenth Edition. Crown 8vo, 5s.

    The Larger Hope. A Sequel to "Salvator Mundi." Second Edition. 16mo, 1s.

    The Genesis of Evil, and other Sermons, mainly expository. Third Edition. Crown 8vo, 6s.

    Balaam. An Exposition and a Study. Crown 8vo, 5s.

    Miracles. An Argument and a Challenge. Crown 8vo, 2s. 6d.

CRAVEN, *Mrs.*—A Year's Meditations. Crown 8vo, 6s.

CRAWFURD, *Oswald.*—Portugal, Old and New. With Illustrations and Maps. New and Cheaper Edition. Crown 8vo, 6s.

CRUISE, *Francis Richard, M.D.*—Thomas à Kempis. Notes of a Visit to the Scenes in which his Life was spent. With Portraits and Illustrations. Demy 8vo, 12s.

Dante: The Banquet (Il Comito). Translated by KATHARINE HILLARD. Crown 8vo.

DARMESTETER, *Arsene.*—The Life of Words as the Symbols of Ideas. Crown 8vo, 4s. 6d.

DAVIDSON, *Rev. Samuel, D.D., LL.D.*—Canon of the Bible; Its Formation, History, and Fluctuations. Third and Revised Edition. Small crown 8vo, 5s.

    The Doctrine of Last Things contained in the New Testament compared with the Notions of the Jews and the Statements of Church Creeds. Small crown 8vo, 3s. 6d.

DAWSON, *Geo., M.A.* Prayers, with a Discourse on Prayer. Edited by his Wife. First Series. Ninth Edition. Small Crown 8vo, 3s. 6d.

    Prayers, with a Discourse on Prayer. Edited by GEORGE ST. CLAIR, F.G.S. Second Series. Small Crown 8vo, 3s. 6d.

    Sermons on Disputed Points and Special Occasions. Edited by his Wife. Fourth Edition. Crown 8vo, 6s.

DAWSON, Geo., M.A.—continued.
> Sermons on Daily Life and Duty. Edited by his Wife. Fifth Edition. Small Crown 8vo, 3s. 6d.
>
> The Authentic Gospel, and other Sermons. Edited by GEORGE ST. CLAIR, F.G.S. Third Edition. Crown 8vo, 6s.
>
> Every-day Counsels. Edited by GEORGE ST. CLAIR, F.G.S. Crown 8vo, 6s.
>
> Biographical Lectures. Edited by GEORGE ST. CLAIR, F.G.S. Third Edition. Large crown 8vo, 7s. 6d.
>
> Shakespeare, and other Lectures. Edited by GEORGE ST. CLAIR, F.G.S. Large crown 8vo, 7s. 6d.

DE JONCOURT, Madame Marie.—Wholesome Cookery. Fourth Edition. Crown 8vo, cloth, 1s. 6d; paper covers, 1s.

DENT, H. C.—A Year in Brazil. With Notes on Religion, Meteorology, Natural History, etc. Maps and Illustrations. Demy 8vo, 18s.

DOWDEN, Edward, LL.D.—Shakspere: a Critical Study of his Mind and Art. Eighth Edition. Post 8vo, 12s.
> Studies in Literature, 1789-1877. Fourth Edition. Large post 8vo, 6s.
>
> Transcripts and Studies. Large post 8vo, 12s.

Dulce Domum. Fcap. 8vo, 5s.

DU MONCEL, Count.—The Telephone, the Microphone, and the Phonograph. With 74 Illustrations. Third Edition. Small crown 8vo, 5s.

DUNN, H. Percy.—Infant Health. The Physiology and Hygiene of Early Life. Crown 8vo. 3s. 6d.

DURUY, Victor.—History of Rome and the Roman People. Edited by Prof. MAHAFFY. With nearly 3000 Illustrations. 4to. 6 vols. in 12 parts, 30s. each vol.

Education Library. Edited by Sir PHILIP MAGNUS:—
> An Introduction to the History of Educational Theories. By OSCAR BROWNING, M.A. Second Edition. 3s. 6d.
>
> Old Greek Education. By the Rev. Prof. MAHAFFY, M.A. Second Edition. 3s. 6d.
>
> School Management. Including a general view of the work of Education, Organization and Discipline. By JOSEPH LANDON. Sixth Edition. 6s.

EDWARDES, Major-General Sir Herbert B.—Memorials of his Life and Letters. By his Wife. With Portrait and Illustrations. 2 vols. Demy 8vo, 36s.

ELSDALE, Henry.—Studies in Tennyson's Idylls. Crown 8vo, 5s.

Eighteenth Century Essays. Selected and Edited by AUSTIN DOBSON. Cheap Edition. Cloth 1s. 6d.

Emerson's (Ralph Waldo) Life. By OLIVER WENDELL HOLMES. English Copyright Edition. With Portrait. Crown 8vo, 6s.

Five o'clock Tea. Containing Receipts for Cakes, Savoury Sandwiches, etc. Fcap. 8vo, cloth, 1s. 6d.; paper covers, 1s.

FLINN, D. Edgar.—Ireland: its Health-Resorts and Watering-Places. With Frontispiece and Maps. Demy 8vo, 5s.

Forbes, Bishop: A Memoir. By the Rev. DONALD J. MACKAY. With Portrait and Map. Crown 8vo, 7s. 6d.

FORDYCE, J.—The New Social Order. Crown 8vo, 3s. 6d.

FOTHERINGHAM, James.—Studies in the Poetry of Robert Browning. Second Edition. Crown 8vo, 6s.

Franklin (Benjamin) as a Man of Letters. By J. B. MACMASTER. Crown 8vo, 5s.

FREWEN, MORETON.—The Economic Crisis. Crown 8vo, 4s. 6d.

From World to Cloister; or, My Novitiate. By BERNARD. Crown 8vo, 5s.

GARDINER, Samuel R., and J. BASS MULLINGER, M.A.—Introduction to the Study of English History. Second Edition. Large crown 8vo, 9s.

Genesis in Advance of Present Science. A Critical Investigation of Chapters I.-IX. By a Septuagenarian Beneficed Presbyter. Demy 8vo, 10s. 6d.

GEORGE, Henry.—Progress and Poverty: An Inquiry into the Causes of Industrial Depressions, and of Increase of Want with Increase of Wealth. The Remedy. Fifth Library Edition. Post 8vo, 7s. 6d. Cabinet Edition. Crown 8vo, 2s. 6d. Also a Cheap Edition. Limp cloth, 1s. 6d.; paper covers, 1s.

    Protection, or Free Trade. An Examination of the Tariff Question, with especial regard to the Interests of Labour. Second Edition. Crown 8vo, 5s.

    Social Problems. Fourth Thousand. Crown 8vo, 5s. Cheap Edition, paper covers, 1s.; cloth 1s. 6d.

GILBERT, Mrs.—Autobiography, and other Memorials. Edited by JOSIAH GILBERT. Fifth Edition. Crown 8vo, 7s. 6d.

GILLMORE, Parker.—Days and Nights by the Desert. Illustrated. Demy 8vo, 10s. 6d.

GLANVILL, Joseph.—Scepsis Scientifica; or, Confest Ignorance, the Way to Science; in an Essay of the Vanity of Dogmatizing and Confident Opinion. Edited, with Introductory Essay, by JOHN OWEN. Elzevir 8vo, printed on hand-made paper, 6s.

GLASS, H. A.—The Story of the Psalters. A History of the Metrical Versions from 1549 to 1885. Crown 8vo, 5s.

Glossary of Terms and Phrases. Edited by the Rev. H. PERCY SMITH and others. Second and Cheaper Edition. Medium 8vo, 7s. 6d.

GLOVER, F., M.A.—Exempla Latina. A First Construing Book, with Short Notes, Lexicon, and an Introduction to the Analysis of Sentences. Second Edition. Fcap. 8vo, 2s.

GOODENOUGH, Commodore J. G.—Memoir of, with Extracts from his Letters and Journals. Edited by his Widow. With Steel Engraved Portrait. Third Edition. Crown 8vo, 5s.

GORDON, Major-General C. G.—His Journals at Kartoum. Printed from the original MS. With Introduction and Notes by A. EGMONT HAKE. Portrait, 2 Maps, and 30 Illustrations. Two vols., demy 8vo, 21s. Also a Cheap Edition in 1 vol., 6s.

   Gordon's (General) Last Journal. A Facsimile of the last Journal received in England from GENERAL GORDON. Reproduced by Photo-lithography. Imperial 4to, £3 3s.

   Events in his Life. From the Day of his Birth to the Day of his Death. By Sir H. W. GORDON. With Maps and Illustrations. Second Edition. Demy 8vo, 7s. 6d.

GOSSE, Edmund.—Seventeenth Century Studies. A Contribution to the History of English Poetry. Demy 8vo, 10s. 6d.

GOULD, Rev. S. Baring, M.A.—Germany, Present and Past. New and Cheaper Edition. Large crown 8vo, 7s. 6d.

   The Vicar of Morwenstow. A Life of Robert Stephen Hawker. Crown 8vo, 5s.

GOWAN, Major Walter E.—A. Ivanoff's Russian Grammar. (16th Edition.) Translated, enlarged, and arranged for use of Students of the Russian Language. Demy 8vo, 6s.

GOWER, Lord Ronald. My Reminiscences. MINIATURE EDITION, printed on hand-made paper, limp parchment antique, 10s. 6d.

   Bric-à-Brac. Being some Photoprints illustrating art objects at Gower Lodge, Windsor. With descriptions. Super royal 8vo. 15s.; extra binding, 21s.

   Last Days of Mary Antoinette. An Historical Sketch. With Portrait and Facsimiles. Fcap. 4to, 10s. 6d.

   Notes of a Tour from Brindisi to Yokohama, 1883-1884. Fcap. 8vo, 2s. 6d.

GRAHAM, William, M.A.—The Creed of Science, Religious, Moral, and Social. Second Edition, Revised. Crown 8vo, 6s.

   The Social Problem, in its Economic, Moral, and Political Aspects. Demy 8vo, 14s.

GRIMLEY, *Rev. H. N., M.A.*—Tremadoc Sermons, chiefly on the Spiritual Body, the Unseen World, and the Divine Humanity. Fourth Edition. Crown 8vo, 6s.

    The Temple of Humanity, and other Sermons. Crown 8vo, 6s.

HADDON, *Caroline.*—The Larger Life, Studies in Hinton's Ethics. Crown 8vo, 5s.

HAECKEL, *Prof. Ernst.*—The History of Creation. Translation revised by Professor E. RAY LANKESTER, M.A., F.R.S. With Coloured Plates and Genealogical Trees of the various groups of both Plants and Animals. 2 vols. Third Edition. Post 8vo, 32s.

    The History of the Evolution of Man. With numerous Illustrations. 2 vols. Post 8vo, 32s.

    A Visit to Ceylon. Post 8vo, 7s. 6d.

    Freedom in Science and Teaching. With a Prefatory Note by T. H. HUXLEY, F.R.S. Crown 8vo, 5s.

HALCOMBE, *J. J.*—Gospel Difficulties due to a Displaced Section of St. Luke. Second Edition. Crown 8vo, 6s.

Hamilton, Memoirs of Arthur, B.A., of Trinity College, Cambridge. Crown 8vo, 6s.

Handbook of Home Rule, being Articles on the Irish Question by Various Writers. Edited by JAMES BRYCE, M.P. Second Edition. Crown 8vo, 1s. sewed, or 1s. 6d. cloth.

HAWEIS, *Rev. H. R., M.A.*—Current Coin. Materialism—The Devil—Crime—Drunkenness—Pauperism—Emotion—Recreation—The Sabbath. Fifth Edition. Crown 8vo, 5s.

    Arrows in the Air. Fifth Edition. Crown 8vo, 5s.

    Speech in Season. Fifth Edition. Crown 8vo, 5s.

    Thoughts for the Times. Fourteenth Edition. Crown 8vo, 5s.

    Unsectarian Family Prayers. New Edition. Fcap. 8vo, 1s. 6d.

HAWTHORNE, *Nathaniel.*—Works. Complete in Twelve Volumes. Large post 8vo, 7s. 6d. each volume.

HEATH, *Francis George.*—Autumnal Leaves. Third and cheaper Edition. Large crown 8vo, 6s.

    Sylvan Winter. With 70 Illustrations. Large crown 8vo, 14s.

HEIDENHAIN, *Rudolph, M.D.*—Hypnotism, or Animal Magnetism. With Preface by G. J. ROMANES. Second Edition. Small crown 8vo, 2s. 6d.

HINTON, *J.*—Life and Letters. With an Introduction by Sir W. W. GULL, Bart., and Portrait engraved on Steel by C. H. Jeens. Fifth Edition. Crown 8vo, 8s. 6d.

HINTON, J.—continued.

    Philosophy and Religion. Selections from the Manuscripts of the late James Hinton. Edited by CAROLINE HADDON. Second Edition. Crown 8vo, 5s.

    The Law Breaker, and The Coming of the Law. Edited by MARGARET HINTON. Crown 8vo, 6s.

    The Mystery of Pain. New Edition. Fcap. 8vo, 1s.

Homer's Iliad. Greek text, with a Translation by J. G. CORDERY. 2 vols. Demy 8vo, 24s.

HOOPER, Mary.—Little Dinners: How to Serve them with Elegance and Economy. Twentieth Edition. Crown 8vo, 2s. 6d.

    Cookery for Invalids, Persons of Delicate Digestion, and Children. Fifth Edition. Crown 8vo, 2s. 6d.

    Every-day Meals. Being Economical and Wholesome Recipes for Breakfast, Luncheon, and Supper. Seventh Edition. Crown 8vo, 2s. 6d.

HOPKINS, Ellice.—Work amongst Working Men. Sixth Edition. Crown 8vo, 3s. 6d.

HORNADAY, W. T.—Two Years in a Jungle. With Illustrations. Demy 8vo, 21s.

HOSPITALIER, E.—The Modern Applications of Electricity. Translated and Enlarged by JULIUS MAIER, Ph.D. 2 vols. Second Edition, Revised, with many additions and numerous Illustrations. Demy 8vo, 25s.

HOWARD, Robert, M.A.—The Church of England and other Religious Communions. A course of Lectures delivered in the Parish Church of Clapham. Crown 8vo, 7s. 6d.

How to Make a Saint; or, The Process of Canonization in the Church of England. By "THE PRIG." Fcap 8vo, 3s. 6d.

HYNDMAN, H. M.—The Historical Basis of Socialism in England. Large crown 8vo, 8s. 6d.

IDDESLEIGH, Earl of.—The Pleasures, Dangers, and Uses of Desultory Reading. Fcap. 8vo, in Whatman paper cover, 1s.

IM THURN, Everard F.—Among the Indians of Guiana. Being Sketches, chiefly anthropologic, from the Interior of British Guiana. With 53 Illustrations and a Map. Demy 8vo, 18s.

Ixora: A Mystery. Crown 8vo, 6s.

Jaunt in a Junk: A Ten Days' Cruise in Indian Seas. Large crown 8vo, 7s. 6d.

JENKINS, E., and RAYMOND, J.—The Architect's Legal Handbook. Third Edition, revised. Crown 8vo, 6s.

JENKINS, Rev. Canon R. C.—**Heraldry: English and Foreign.** With a Dictionary of Heraldic Terms and 156 Illustrations. Small crown 8vo, 3s. 6d.

Jerome, St., Life. By M. J. MARTIN. Large crown 8vo, 6s.

JOEL, L.—**A Consul's Manual and Shipowner's and Shipmaster's Practical Guide in their Transactions Abroad.** With Definitions of Nautical, Mercantile, and Legal Terms; a Glossary of Mercantile Terms in English, French, German, Italian, and Spanish; Tables of the Money, Weights, and Measures of the Principal Commercial Nations and their Equivalents in British Standards; and Forms of Consular and Notarial Acts. Demy 8vo, 12s.

JOHNSTON, H. H., F.Z.S.—**The Kilima-njaro Expedition.** A Record of Scientific Exploration in Eastern Equatorial Africa, and a General Description of the Natural History, Languages, and Commerce of the Kilima-njaro District. With 6 Maps, and over 80 Illustrations by the Author. Demy 8vo, 21s.

JORDAN, Furneaux, F.R.C.S.—**Anatomy and Physiology in Character.** Crown 8vo, 5s.

KAUFMANN, Rev. M., M.A.—**Socialism: its Nature, its Dangers, and its Remedies considered.** Crown 8vo, 7s. 6d.

    Utopias; or, Schemes of Social Improvement, from Sir Thomas More to Karl Marx. Crown 8vo, 5s.

    Christian Socialism. Crown 8vo, 4s. 6d.

KAY, David, F.R.G.S.—**Education and Educators.** Crown 8vo, 7s. 6d.

    Memory: what it is and how to improve it. Crown 8vo, 6s.

KAY, Joseph.—**Free Trade in Land.** Edited by his Widow. With Preface by the Right Hon. JOHN BRIGHT, M.P. Seventh Edition. Crown 8vo, 5s.

    *** Also a cheaper edition, without the Appendix, but with a Review of Recent Changes in the Land Laws of England, by the RIGHT HON. G. OSBORNE MORGAN, Q.C., M.P. Cloth, 1s. 6d.; paper covers, 1s.

KELKE, W. H. H.—**An Epitome of English Grammar for the Use of Students.** Adapted to the London Matriculation Course and Similar Examinations. Crown 8vo, 4s. 6d.

KEMPIS, Thomas à.—**Of the Imitation of Christ.** Parchment Library Edition.—Parchment or cloth, 6s.; vellum, 7s. 6d. The Red Line Edition, fcap. 8vo, cloth extra, 2s. 6d. The Cabinet Edition, small 8vo, cloth limp, 1s.; cloth boards, 1s. 6d. The Miniature Edition, cloth limp, 32mo, 1s.; or with red lines, 1s. 6d.

    *** All the above Editions may be had in various extra bindings.

KEMPIS, Thomas à—continued.

    Notes of a Visit to the Scenes in which his Life was spent. With numerous Illustrations. By F. R. CRUISE, M.D. Demy 8vo, 12s.

KENDALL, Henry.—The Kinship of Men. An argument from Pedigrees, or Genealogy viewed as a Science. With Diagrams. Crown 8vo, 5s.

KENNARD, Rev. R. B.—A Manual of Confirmation. 18mo. Sewed, 3d.; cloth, 1s.

KIDD, Joseph, M.D.—The Laws of Therapeutics; or, the Science and Art of Medicine. Second Edition. Crown 8vo, 6s.

KINGSFORD, Anna, M.D.—The Perfect Way in Diet. A Treatise advocating a Return to the Natural and Ancient Food of our Race. Third Edition. Small crown 8vo, 2s.

KINGSLEY, Charles, M.A.—Letters and Memories of his Life. Edited by his Wife. With two Steel Engraved Portraits, and Vignettes on Wood. Sixteenth Cabinet Edition. 2 vols. Crown 8vo, 12s.

    ** Also a People's Edition, in one volume. With Portrait. Crown 8vo, 6s.

    All Saints' Day, and other Sermons. Edited by the Rev. W. HARRISON. Third Edition. Crown 8vo, 7s. 6d.

    True Words for Brave Men. A Book for Soldiers' and Sailors' Libraries. Sixteenth Thousand. Crown 8vo, 2s. 6d.

KNOX, Alexander A.—The New Playground; or, Wanderings in Algeria. New and Cheaper Edition. Large crown 8vo, 6s.

Land Concentration and Irresponsibility of Political Power, as causing the Anomaly of a Widespread State of Want by the Side of the Vast Supplies of Nature. Crown 8vo, 5s.

LANDON, Joseph.—School Management; Including a General View of the Work of Education, Organization, and Discipline. Sixth Edition. Crown 8vo, 6s.

LAURIE, S. S.—The Rise and Early Constitution of Universities. With a Survey of Mediæval Education. Crown 8vo, 6s.

LEFEVRE, Right Hon. G. Shaw.—Peel and O'Connell. Demy 8vo, 10s. 6d.

    Incidents of Coercion. A Journal of two visits to Loughrea. Crown 8vo.

    Letters from an Unknown Friend. By the Author of "Charles Lowder." With a Preface by the Rev. W. H. CLEAVER. Fcap. 8vo, 1s.

Life of a Prig. By ONE. Third Edition. Fcap. 8vo, 3s. 6d.

LILLIE, Arthur, M.R.A.S.—The Popular Life of Buddha. Containing an Answer to the Hibbert Lectures of 1881. With Illustrations. Crown 8vo, 6s.

LILLIE, Arthur, M.R.A.S.—continued.

    Buddhism in Christendom ; or, Jesus the Essene. With Illustrations. Demy 8vo, 15s.

LOCHER, Carl.—An Explanation of Organ Stops, with Hints for Effective Combinations. Demy 8vo, 5s.

LONGFELLOW, H. Wadsworth.—Life. By his Brother, SAMUEL LONGFELLOW. With Portraits and Illustrations. 3 vols. Demy 8vo, 42s.

LONSDALE, Margaret.—Sister Dora : a Biography. With Portrait. Twenty-ninth Edition. Small crown 8vo, 2s. 6d.

    George Eliot: Thoughts upon her Life, her Books, and Herself. Second Edition. Small crown 8vo, 1s. 6d.

LOUNSBURY, Thomas R.—James Fenimore Cooper. With Portrait. Crown 8vo, 5s.

LOWDER, Charles.—A Biography. By the Author of "St. Teresa." Twelfth Edition. Crown 8vo. With Portrait. 3s. 6d.

LÜCKES, Eva C. E.—Lectures on General Nursing, delivered to the Probationers of the London Hospital Training School for Nurses. Second Edition. Crown 8vo, 2s. 6d.

LYTTON, Edward Bulwer, Lord.—Life, Letters and Literary Remains. By his Son, the EARL OF LYTTON. With Portraits, Illustrations and Facsimiles. Demy 8vo. Vols. I. and II., 32s.

MACHIAVELLI, Niccolò.— Life and Times. By Prof. VILLARI. Translated by LINDA VILLARI. 4 vols. Large post 8vo, 48s.

    Discourses on the First Decade of Titus Livius. Translated from the Italian by NINIAN HILL THOMSON, M.A. Large crown 8vo, 12s.

    The Prince. Translated from the Italian by N. H. T. Small crown 8vo, printed on hand-made paper, bevelled boards, 6s.

MACNEILL, J. G. Swift.—How the Union was carried. Crown 8vo, cloth, 1s. 6d. ; paper covers, 1s.

MAGNUS, Lady.—About the Jews since Bible Times. From the Babylonian Exile till the English Exodus. Small crown 8vo, 6s.

Maintenon, Madame de. By EMILY BOWLES. With Portrait, Large crown 8vo, 7s. 6d.

Many Voices. A volume of Extracts from the Religious Writers of Christendom from the First to the Sixteenth Century. With Biographical Sketches. Crown 8vo, cloth extra, red edges, 6s.

MARKHAM, Capt. Albert Hastings, R.N.—The Great Frozen Sea : A Personal Narrative of the Voyage of the *Alert* during the Arctic Expedition of 1875-6. With 6 full-page Illustrations, 2 Maps, and 27 Woodcuts. Sixth and Cheaper Edition. Crown 8vo, 6s.

MARTINEAU, Gertrude.—Outline Lessons on Morals. Small crown 8vo, 3s. 6d.

MASON, Charlotte M.—Home Education: a Course of Lectures to Ladies. Crown 8vo, 3s. 6d.

Matter and Energy: An Examination of the Fundamental Conceptions of Physical Force. By B. L. L. Small crown 8vo, 2s.

MATUCE, H. Ogram. A Wanderer. Crown 8vo, 5s.

MAUDSLEY, H., M.D.—Body and Will. Being an Essay concerning Will, in its Metaphysical, Physiological, and Pathological Aspects. 8vo, 12s.

    Natural Causes and Supernatural Seemings. Second Edition. Crown 8vo, 6s.

McGRATH, Terence.—Pictures from Ireland. New and Cheaper Edition. Crown 8vo, 2s.

McKINNEY, S. B. G.—Science and Art of Religion. Crown 8vo, 8s. 6d.

MEREDITH, M.A.—Theotokos, the Example for Woman. Dedicated, by permission, to Lady Agnes Wood. Revised by the Venerable Archdeacon DENISON. 32mo, limp cloth, 1s. 6d.

MILLER, Edward.—The History and Doctrines of Irvingism; or, The so-called Catholic and Apostolic Church. 2 vols. Large post 8vo, 15s.

    The Church in Relation to the State. Large crown 8vo, 4s.

MILLS, Herbert.—Poverty and the State; or, Work for the Unemployed. An Inquiry into the Causes and Extent of Enforced Idleness, with a Statement of a Remedy. Crown 8vo, 6s.

Mitchel, John, Life. By WILLIAM DILLON. 2 vols. 8vo. With Portrait. 21s.

MITCHELL, Lucy M.—A History of Ancient Sculpture. With numerous Illustrations, including 6 Plates in Phototype. Super-royal 8vo, 42s.

MOCKLER, E.—A Grammar of the Baloochee Language, as it is spoken in Makran (Ancient Gedrosia), in the Persia-Arabic and Roman characters. Fcap. 8vo, 5s.

MOHL, Julius and Mary.—Letters and Recollections of. By M. C. M. SIMPSON. With Portraits and Two Illustrations. Demy 8vo, 15s.

MOLESWORTH, Rev. W. Nassau, M.A.—History of the Church of England from 1660. Large crown 8vo, 7s. 6d.

MORELL, J. R.—Euclid Simplified in Method and Language. Being a Manual of Geometry. Compiled from the most important French Works, approved by the University of Paris and the Minister of Public Instruction. Fcap. 8vo, 2s. 6d.

MORISON, *J. Cotter.*—The Service of Man: an Essay towards the Religion of the Future. Crown 8vo, 5s.

MORSE, *E. S., Ph.D.*—First Book of Zoology. With numerous Illustrations. New and Cheaper Edition. Crown 8vo, 2s. 6d.

My Lawyer: A Concise Abridgment of the Laws of England. By a Barrister-at-Law. Crown 8vo, 6s. 6d.

NELSON, *J. H., M.A.*—A Prospectus of the Scientific Study of the Hindû Law. Demy 8vo, 9s.

    Indian Usage and Judge-made Law in Madras. Demy 8vo, 12s.

NEWMAN, *Cardinal.*—Characteristics from the Writings of. Being Selections from his various Works. Arranged with the Author's personal Approval. Seventh Edition. With Portrait. Crown 8vo, 6s.

    *** A Portrait of Cardinal Newman, mounted for framing, can be had, 2s. 6d.

NEWMAN, *Francis William.*—Essays on Diet. Small crown 8vo, cloth limp, 2s.

    Miscellanies. Vol. II. Essays, Tracts, and Addresses, Moral and Religious. Demy 8vo, 12s.

    Reminiscences of Two Exiles and Two Wars. Crown 8vo.

New Social Teachings. By POLITICUS. Small crown 8vo, 5s.

NICOLS, *Arthur, F.G.S., F.R.G.S.*—Chapters from the Physical History of the Earth: an Introduction to Geology and Palæontology. With numerous Illustrations. Crown 8vo, 5s.

NIHILL, *Rev. H. D.*—The Sisters of St. Mary at the Cross: Sisters of the Poor and their Work. Crown 8vo, 2s. 6d.

NOEL, *The Hon. Roden.*—Essays on Poetry and Poets. Demy 8vo, 12s.

NOPS, *Marianne.*—Class Lessons on Euclid. Part I. containing the First Two Books of the Elements. Crown 8vo, 2s. 6d.

Nuces: EXERCISES ON THE SYNTAX OF THE PUBLIC SCHOOL LATIN PRIMER. New Edition in Three Parts. Crown 8vo, each 1s.

    *** The Three Parts can also be had bound together, 3s.

OATES, *Frank, F.R.G.S.*—Matabele Land and the Victoria Falls. A Naturalist's Wanderings in the Interior of South Africa. Edited by C. G. OATES, B.A. With numerous Illustrations and 4 Maps. Demy 8vo, 21s.

O'BRIEN, *R. Barry.*—Irish Wrongs and English Remedies, with other Essays. Crown 8vo, 5s.

C

OLIVER, *Robert.*—Unnoticed Analogies. A Talk on the Irish Question. Crown 8vo.

O'MEARA, *Kathleen.*—Henri Perreyve and his Counsels to the Sick. Small crown 8vo, 5s.

One and a Half in Norway. A Chronicle of Small Beer. By Either and Both. Small crown 8vo, 3s. 6d.

O'NEIL, *the late Rev. Lord.*—Sermons. With Memoir and Portrait. Crown 8vo, 6s.

Essays and Addresses. Crown 8vo, 5s.

OTTLEY, *H. Bickersteth.*—The Great Dilemma. Christ His Own Witness or His Own Accuser. Six Lectures. Second Edition. Crown 8vo, 3s. 6d.

Our Priests and their Tithes. By a Priest of the Province of Canterbury. Crown 8vo, 5s.

Our Public Schools—Eton, Harrow, Winchester, Rugby, Westminster, Marlborough, The Charterhouse. Crown 8vo, 6s.

PALMER, *the late William.*—Notes of a Visit to Russia in 1840-1841. Selected and arranged by JOHN H. CARDINAL NEWMAN, with Portrait. Crown 8vo, 8s. 6d.

Early Christian Symbolism. A Series of Compositions from Fresco Paintings, Glasses, and Sculptured Sarcophagi. Edited by the Rev. Provost NORTHCOTE, D.D., and the Rev. Canon BROWNLOW, M.A. With Coloured Plates, folio, 42s., or with Plain Plates, folio, 25s.

Parchment Library. Choicely Printed on hand-made paper, limp parchment antique or cloth, 6s. ; vellum, 7s. 6d. each volume.

Sartor Resartus. By THOMAS CARLYLE.

The Poetical Works of John Milton. 2 vols.

Chaucer's Canterbury Tales. Edited by A. W. POLLARD. 2 vols.

Letters and Journals of Jonathan Swift. Selected and edited, with a Commentary and Notes, by STANLEY LANE POOLE.

De Quincey's Confessions of an English Opium Eater. Reprinted from the First Edition. Edited by RICHARD GARNETT.

The Gospel according to Matthew, Mark, and Luke.

Selections from the Prose Writings of Jonathan Swift. With a Preface and Notes by STANLEY LANE-POOLE and Portrait.

English Sacred Lyrics.

Sir Joshua Reynolds's Discourses. Edited by EDMUND GOSSE.

Parchment Library—*continued*.

- **Selections from Milton's Prose Writings.** Edited by ERNEST MYERS.
- **The Book of Psalms.** Translated by the Rev. Canon T. K. CHEYNE, M.A., D.D.
- **The Vicar of Wakefield.** With Preface and Notes by AUSTIN DOBSON.
- **English Comic Dramatists.** Edited by OSWALD CRAWFURD.
- **English Lyrics.**
- **The Sonnets of John Milton.** Edited by MARK PATTISON. With Portrait after Vertue.
- **French Lyrics.** Selected and Annotated by GEORGE SAINTSBURY. With a Miniature Frontispiece designed and etched by H. G. Glindoni.
- **Fables by Mr. John Gay.** With Memoir by AUSTIN DOBSON, and an Etched Portrait from an unfinished Oil Sketch by Sir Godfrey Kneller.
- **Select Letters of Percy Bysshe Shelley.** Edited, with an Introduction, by RICHARD GARNETT.
- **The Christian Year.** Thoughts in Verse for the Sundays and Holy Days throughout the Year. With Miniature Portrait of the Rev. J. Keble, after a Drawing by G. Richmond, R.A.
- **Shakspere's Works.** Complete in Twelve Volumes.
- **Eighteenth Century Essays.** Selected and Edited by AUSTIN DOBSON. With a Miniature Frontispiece by R. Caldecott.
- **Q. Horati Flacci Opera.** Edited by F. A. CORNISH, Assistant Master at Eton. With a Frontispiece after a design by L. Alma Tadema, etched by Leopold Lowenstam.
- **Edgar Allan Poe's Poems.** With an Essay on his Poetry by ANDREW LANG, and a Frontispiece by Linley Sambourne.
- **Shakspere's Sonnets.** Edited by EDWARD DOWDEN. With a Frontispiece etched by Leopold Lowenstam, after the Death Mask.
- **English Odes.** Selected by EDMUND GOSSE. With Frontispiece on India paper by Hamo Thornycroft, A.R.A.
- **Of the Imitation of Christ.** By THOMAS À KEMPIS. A revised Translation. With Frontispiece on India paper, from a Design by W. B. Richmond.
- **Poems:** Selected from PERCY BYSSHE SHELLEY. Dedicated to Lady Shelley. With a Preface by RICHARD GARNETT and a Miniature Frontispiece.

PARSLOE, Joseph.—**Our Railways.** Sketches, Historical and Descriptive. With Practical Information as to Fares and Rates, etc., and a Chapter on Railway Reform. Crown 8vo, 6s.

PASCAL, Blaise.—**The Thoughts of.** Translated from the Text of Auguste Molinier, by C. KEGAN PAUL. Large crown 8vo, with Frontispiece, printed on hand-made paper, parchment antique, or cloth, 12s.; vellum, 15s. New Edition. Crown 8vo, 6s.

PATON, W. A.—**Down the Islands.** A Voyage to the Caribbees. With Illustration. Medium 8vo, 16s.

PAUL, C. Kegan.—**Biographical Sketches.** Printed on hand-made paper, bound in buckram. Second Edition. Crown 8vo, 7s. 6d.

PEARSON, Rev. S.—**Week-day Living.** A Book for Young Men and Women. Second Edition. Crown 8vo, 5s.

PENRICE, Major J.—**Arabic and English Dictionary of the Koran.** 4to, 21s.

PESCHEL, Dr. Oscar.—**The Races of Man and their Geographical Distribution.** Second Edition. Large crown 8vo, 9s.

PIDGEON, D.—**An Engineer's Holiday;** or, Notes of a Round Trip from Long. 0° to 0°. New and Cheaper Edition. Large crown 8vo, 7s. 6d.

Old World Questions and New World Answers. Second Edition. Large crown 8vo, 7s. 6d.

Plain Thoughts for Men. Eight Lectures delivered at Forester's Hall, Clerkenwell, during the London Mission, 1884. Crown 8vo, cloth, 1s. 6d; paper covers, 1s.

PLOWRIGHT, C. B.—**The British Uredineæ and Ustilagineæ.** With Illustrations. Demy 8vo, 10s. 6d.

PRICE, Prof. Bonamy.—**Chapters on Practical Political Economy.** Being the Substance of Lectures delivered before the University of Oxford. New and Cheaper Edition. Crown 8vo, 5s.

Prig's Bede: the Venerable Bede, Expurgated, Expounded, and Exposed. By "THE PRIG." Second Edition. Fcap. 8vo, 3s. 6d.

Pulpit Commentary, The. (*Old Testament Series.*) Edited by the Rev. J. S. EXELL, M.A., and the Very Rev. Dean H. D. M. SPENCE, M.A., D.D.

    Genesis. By the Rev. T. WHITELAW, D.D. With Homilies by the Very Rev. J. F. MONTGOMERY, D.D., Rev. Prof. R. A. REDFORD, M.A., LL.B., Rev. F. HASTINGS, Rev. W. ROBERTS, M.A. An Introduction to the Study of the Old Testament by the Venerable Archdeacon FARRAR, D.D., F.R.S.; and Introductions to the Pentateuch by the Right Rev. H. COTTERILL, D.D., and Rev. T. WHITELAW, M.A. Eighth Edition. 1 vol., 15s.

Kegan Paul, Trench & Co.'s Publications.   21

Pulpit Commentary, The—*continued.*

    Exodus. By the Rev. Canon RAWLINSON. With Homilies by Rev. J. ORR, D.D., Rev. D. YOUNG, B.A., Rev. C. A. GOODHART, Rev. J. URQUHART, and the Rev. H. T. ROBJOHNS. Fourth Edition. 2 vols., 9s. each.

    Leviticus. By the Rev. Prebendary MEYRICK, M.A. With Introductions by the Rev. R. COLLINS, Rev. Professor A. CAVE, and Homilies by Rev. Prof. REDFORD, LL.B., Rev. J. A. MACDONALD, Rev. W. CLARKSON, B.A., Rev. S. R. ALDRIDGE, LL.B., and Rev. McCHEYNE EDGAR. Fourth Edition. 15s.

    Numbers. By the Rev. R. WINTERBOTHAM, LL.B. With Homilies by the Rev. Professor W. BINNIE, D.D., Rev. E. S. PROUT, M.A., Rev. D. YOUNG, Rev. J. WAITE, and an Introduction by the Rev. THOMAS WHITELAW, M.A. Fifth Edition. 15s.

    Deuteronomy. By the Rev. W. L. ALEXANDER, D.D. With Homilies by Rev. C. CLEMANCE, D.D., Rev. J. ORR, D.D., Rev. R. M. EDGAR, M.A., Rev. D. DAVIES, M.A. Fourth edition. 15s.

    Joshua. By Rev. J. J. LIAS, M.A. With Homilies by Rev. S. R. ALDRIDGE, LL.B., Rev. R. GLOVER, REV. E. DE PRESSENSÉ, D.D., Rev. J. WAITE, B.A., Rev. W. F. ADENEY, M.A.; and an Introduction by the Rev. A. PLUMMER, M.A. Fifth Edition. 12s. 6d.

    Judges and Ruth. By the Bishop of BATH and WELLS, and Rev. J. MORISON, D.D. With Homilies by Rev. A. F. MUIR, M.A., Rev. W. F. ADENEY, M.A., Rev. W. M. STATHAM, and Rev. Professor J. THOMSON, M.A. Fifth Edition. 10s. 6d.

    1 Samuel. By the Very Rev. R. P. SMITH, D.D. With Homilies by Rev. DONALD FRASER, D.D., Rev. Prof. CHAPMAN, and Rev. B. DALE. Sixth Edition. 15s.

    1 Kings. By the Rev. JOSEPH HAMMOND, LL.B. With Homilies by the Rev. E. DE PRESSENSÉ, D.D., Rev. J. WAITE, B.A., Rev. A. ROWLAND, LL.B., Rev. J. A. MACDONALD, and Rev. J. URQUHART. Fifth Edition. 15s.

    1 Chronicles. By the Rev. Prof. P. C. BARKER, M.A., LL.B. With Homilies by Rev. Prof. J. R. THOMSON, M.A., Rev. R. TUCK, B.A., Rev. W. CLARKSON, B.A., Rev. F. WHITFIELD, M.A., and Rev. RICHARD GLOVER. 15s.

    Ezra, Nehemiah, and Esther. By Rev. Canon G. RAWLINSON, M.A. With Homilies by Rev. Prof. J. R. THOMSON, M.A., Rev. Prof. R. A. REDFORD, LL.B., M.A., Rev. W. S. LEWIS, M.A., Rev. J. A. MACDONALD, Rev. A. MACKENNAL, B.A., Rev. W. CLARKSON, B.A., Rev. F. HASTINGS, Rev. W. DINWIDDIE, LL.B., Rev. Prof. ROWLANDS, B.A., Rev. G. WOOD, B.A., Rev. Prof. P. C. BARKER, M.A., LL.B., and the Rev. J. S. EXELL, M.A. Sixth Edition. 1 vol., 12s. 6d.

Pulpit Commentary, The—*continued.*

> Isaiah. By the Rev. Canon G. RAWLINSON, M.A. With Homilies by Rev. Prof. E. JOHNSON, M.A., Rev. W. CLARKSON, B.A., Rev. W. M. STATHAM, and Rev. R. TUCK, B.A. Second Edition. 2 vols., 15*s.* each.
>
> Jeremiah. (Vol. I.) By the Rev. Canon T. K. CHEYNE, D.D. With Homilies by the Rev. W. F. ADENEY, M.A., Rev. A. F. MUIR, M.A., Rev. S. CONWAY, B.A., Rev. J. WAITE, B.A., and Rev. D. YOUNG, B.A. Third Edition. 15*s.*
>
> Jeremiah (Vol. II.) and Lamentations. By Rev. Canon T. K. CHEYNE, D.D. With Homilies by Rev. Prof. J. R. THOMSON, M.A., Rev. W. F. ADENEY, M.A., Rev. A. F. MUIR, M.A., Rev. S. CONWAY, B.A., Rev. D. YOUNG, B.A. 15*s.*
>
> Hosea and Joel. By the Rev. Prof. J. J. GIVEN, Ph.D., D.D. With Homilies by the Rev. Prof. J. R. THOMSON, M.A., Rev. A. ROWLAND, B.A., LL.B., Rev. C. JERDAN, M.A., LL.B., Rev. J. ORR, D.D., and Rev. D. THOMAS, D.D. 15*s.*

Pulpit Commentary, The. (*New Testament Series.*)

> St. Mark. By Very Rev. E. BICKERSTETH, D.D., Dean of Lichfield. With Homilies by Rev. Prof. THOMSON, M.A., Rev. Prof. J. J. GIVEN, Ph.D., D.D., Rev. Prof. JOHNSON, M.A., Rev. A. ROWLAND, B.A., LL.B., Rev. A. MUIR, and Rev. R. GREEN. Fifth Edition. 2 vols., 10*s.* 6*d.* each.
>
> St. John. By Rev. Prof. H. R. REYNOLDS, D.D. With Homilies by Rev. Prof. T. CROSKERY, D.D., Rev. Prof J. R. THOMSON, M.A., Rev. D. YOUNG, B.A., Rev. B. THOMAS, Rev. G. BROWN. Second Edition. 2 vols. 15*s.* each.
>
> The Acts of the Apostles. By the Bishop of BATH and WELLS. With Homilies by Rev. Prof. P. C. BARKER, M.A., LL.B., Rev. Prof. F. JOHNSON, M.A., Rev. Prof. R. A. REDFORD, LL.B., Rev. R. TUCK, B.A., Rev. W. CLARKSON, B.A. Fourth Edition. 2 vols., 10*s.* 6*d.* each.
>
> 1 Corinthians. By the Ven. Archdeacon FARRAR, D.D. With Homilies by Rev. Ex-Chancellor LIPSCOMB, LL.D., Rev. DAVID THOMAS, D.D., Rev. D. FRASER, D.D., Rev. Prof. J. R. THOMSON, M.A., Rev. J. WAITE, B.A., Rev. R. TUCK, B.A., Rev. E. HURNDALL, M.A., and Rev. H. BREMNER, B.D. Fourth Edition. 15*s.*
>
> 2 Corinthians and Galatians. By the Ven. Archdeacon FARRAR, D.D., and Rev. Prebendary E. HUXTABLE. With Homilies by Rev. Ex-Chancellor LIPSCOMB, LL.D., Rev. DAVID THOMAS, D.D., Rev. DONALD FRASER, D.D., Rev. R. TUCK, B.A., Rev. E. HURNDALL, M.A., Rev. Prof. J. R. THOMSON, M.A., Rev. R. FINLAYSON, B.A., Rev. W. F. ADENEY, M.A., Rev. R. M. EDGAR, M.A., and Rev. T. CROSKERY, D.D. Second Edition. 21*s.*

Pulpit Commentary, The.—*continued.*

> **Ephesians, Philippians, and Colossians.** By the Rev. Prof. W. G. BLAIKIE, D.D., Rev. B. C. CAFFIN, M.A., and Rev. G. G. FINDLAY, B.A. With Homilies by Rev. D. THOMAS, D.D., Rev. R. M. EDGAR, M.A., Rev. R. FINLAYSON, B.A., Rev. W. F. ADENEY, M.A., Rev. Prof. T. CROSKERY, D.D., Rev. F. S. PROUT, M.A., Rev. Canon VERNON HUTTON, and Rev. U. R. THOMAS, D.D. Second Edition. 21s.

> **Thessalonians, Timothy, Titus, and Philemon.** By the Bishop of Bath and Wells, Rev. Dr. GLOAG and Rev. Dr. EALES. With Homilies by the Rev. B. C. CAFFIN, M.A., Rev. R. FINLAYSON, B.A., Rev. Prof. T. CROSKERY, D.D., Rev. W. F. ADENEY, M.A., Rev. W. M. STATHAM, and Rev. D. THOMAS, D.D. 15s.

> **Hebrews and James.** By the Rev. J. BARMBY, D.D., and Rev Prebendary E. C. S. GIBSON, M.A. With Homiletics by the Rev. C. JERDAN, M.A., LL.B., and Rev. Prebendary E. C. S. GIBSON. And Homilies by the Rev. W. JONES, Rev. C. NEW, Rev. D. YOUNG, B.A., Rev. J. S. BRIGHT, Rev. T. F. LOCKYER, B.A., and Rev. C. JERDAN, M.A., LL.B. Second Edition. 15s.

PUSEY, Dr.—**Sermons for the Church's Seasons from Advent to Trinity.** Selected from the Published Sermons of the late EDWARD BOUVERIE PUSEY, D.D. Crown 8vo, 5s.

QUEKETT, Rev. W.—**My Sayings and Doings.** With Reminiscences of my Life. With Illustrations. Demy 8vo, 18s.

RANKE, Leopold von.—**Universal History.** The oldest Historical Group of Nations and the Greeks. Edited by G. W. PROTHERO. Demy 8vo, 16s.

RENDELL, J. M.—**Concise Handbook of the Island of Madeira.** With Plan of Funchal and Map of the Island. Fcap. 8vo, 1s. 6d.

REVELL, W. F.—**Ethical Forecasts.** Crown 8vo, 3s. 6d.

REYNOLDS, Rev. J. W.—**The Supernatural in Nature.** A Verification by Free Use of Science. Third Edition, Revised and Enlarged. Demy 8vo, 14s.

> **The Mystery of Miracles.** Third and Enlarged Edition. Crown 8vo, 6s.

> **The Mystery of the Universe our Common Faith.** Demy 8vo, 14s.

> **The World to Come:** Immortality a Physical Fact. Crown 8vo, 6s.

RIBOT, Prof. Th.—**Heredity:** A Psychological Study of its Phenomena, its Laws, its Causes, and its Consequences. Second Edition. Large crown 8vo, 9s.

RIVINGTON, Luke.—**Authority, or a Plain Reason for joining the Church of Rome.** Crown 8vo., 3s. 6d.

ROBERTSON, The late Rev. F. W., M.A.—**Life and Letters of.** Edited by the Rev. STOPFORD BROOKE, M.A.
    I. Two vols., uniform with the Sermons. With Steel Portrait. Crown 8vo, 7s. 6d.
    II. Library Edition, in Demy 8vo, with Portrait. 12s.
    III. A Popular Edition, in 1 vol. Crown 8vo, 6s.

Sermons. Four Series. Small crown 8vo, 3s. 6d. each.

The Human Race, and other Sermons. Preached at Cheltenham, Oxford, and Brighton. New and Cheaper Edition. Small crown 8vo, 3s. 6d.

Notes on Genesis. New and Cheaper Edition. Small crown 8vo, 3s. 6d.

Expository Lectures on St. Paul's Epistles to the Corinthians. A New Edition. Small crown 8vo, 5s.

Lectures and Addresses, with other Literary Remains. A New Edition. Small crown 8vo, 5s.

An Analysis of Tennyson's "In Memoriam." (Dedicated by Permission to the Poet-Laureate.) Fcap. 8vo, 2s.

The Education of the Human Race. Translated from the German of GOTTHOLD EPHRAIM LESSING. Fcap. 8vo, 2s. 6d.

The above Works can also be had, bound in half morocco.

⁂ A Portrait of the late Rev. F. W. Robertson, mounted for framing, can be had, 2s. 6d.

ROGERS, William.—**Reminiscences.** Compiled by R. H. HADDEN. With Portrait. Crown 8vo, 6s.

ROMANES, G. J.—**Mental Evolution in Animals.** With a Posthumous Essay on Instinct by CHARLES DARWIN, F.R.S. Demy 8vo, 12s.

ROSMINI SERBATI, Antonio.—**Life.** By the REV. W. LOCKHART. Second Edition. 2 vols. With Portraits. Crown 8vo, 12s.

ROSS, Janet.—**Italian Sketches.** With 14 full-page Illustrations. Crown 8vo, 7s. 6d.

RULE, Martin, M.A.—**The Life and Times of St. Anselm, Archbishop of Canterbury and Primate of the Britains.** 2 vols. Demy 8vo, 32s.

SAVERY, C. E.—**The Church of England; an Historical Sketch.** Crown 8vo.

SAYCE, Rev. Archibald Henry.—**Introduction to the Science of Language.** 2 vols. Second Edition. Large post 8vo, 21s.

SCOONES, W. Baptiste.—**Four Centuries of English Letters:** A Selection of 350 Letters by 150 Writers, from the Period of the Paston Letters to the Present Time. Third Edition. Large crown 8vo, 6s.

SEYMOUR, W. Digby, Q.C.,—Home Rule and State Supremacy. Crown 8vo, 3s 6d.

Shakspere's Works. The Avon Edition, 12 vols., fcap. 8vo, cloth, 18s.; in cloth box, 21s.; bound in 6 vols., cloth, 15s.

Shakspere's Works, an Index to. By EVANGELINE O'CONNOR. Crown 8vo, 5s.

SHELLEY, Percy Bysshe.—Life. By EDWARD DOWDEN, LL.D. 2 vols. With Portraits. Demy 8vo, 36s.

SHILLITO, Rev. Joseph.—Womanhood: its Duties, Temptations and Privileges. A Book for Young Women. Third Edition. Crown 8vo, 3s. 6d.

Shooting, Practical Hints on. Being a Treatise on the Shot Gun and its Management. By "20 Bore." With 55 Illustrations. Demy 8vo, 12s.

Sister Augustine, Superior of the Sisters of Charity at the St. Johannis Hospital at Bonn. Authorized Translation by HANS THARAU, from the German "Memorials of AMALIE VON LASAULX." Cheap Edition. Large crown 8vo, 4s. 6d.

※ SKINNER, James.—A Memoir. By the Author of "Charles Lowder." With a Preface by the Rev. Canon CARTER, and Portrait. Large crown, 7s. 6d.
※⁎※ Also a cheap Edition. With Portrait. Fourth Edition. Crown 8vo, 3s. 6d.

SMEATON, D. Mackenzie.—The Loyal Karens of Burma. Crown 8vo, 4s. 6d.

SMITH, Edward, M.D., LL.B., F.R.S.—Tubercular Consumption in its Early and Remediable Stages. Second Edition. Crown 8vo, 6s.

SMITH, L. A.—The Music of the Waters: Sailor's Chanties and Working Songs of the Sea. Demy 8vo.

Spanish Mystics. By the Editor of "Many Voices." Crown 8vo, 5s.

Specimens of English Prose Style from Malory to Macaulay. Selected and Annotated, with an Introductory Essay, by GEORGE SAINTSBURY. Large crown 8vo, printed on handmade paper, parchment antique or cloth, 12s.; vellum, 15s.

Stray Papers on Education, and Scenes from School Life. By B. H. Second Edition. Small crown 8vo, 3s. 6d.

STREATFEILD, Rev. G. S., M.A.—Lincolnshire and the Danes. Large crown 8vo, 7s. 6d.

STRECKER-WISLICENUS.—Organic Chemistry. Translated and Edited, with Extensive Additions, by W. R. HODGKINSON, Ph.D., and A. J. GREENAWAY, F.I.C. Second and cheaper Edition. Demy 8vo, 12s. 6d.

Suakin, 1885; being a Sketch of the Campaign of this year. By an Officer who was there. Second Edition. Crown 8vo, 2s. 6d.

SULLY, *James, M.A.*—Pessimism : a History and a Criticism. Second Edition. Demy 8vo, 14s.

SWANWICK, *Anna.*—An Utopian Dream, and how it may be Realized. Fcap. 8vo, 1s.

SWEDENBORG, *Eman.*—De Cultu et Amore Dei ubi Agitur de Telluris ortu, Paradiso et Vivario, tum de Primogeniti Seu Adami Nativitate Infantia, et Amore. Crown 8vo, 6s.

On the Worship and Love of God. Treating of the Birth of the Earth, Paradise, and the Abode of Living Creatures. Translated from the original Latin. Crown 8vo, 7s. 6d.

Prodromus Philosophiæ Ratiocinantis de Infinito, et Causa Finali Creationis : deque Mechanismo Operationis Animæ et Corporis. Edidit THOMAS MURRAY GORMAN, M.A. Crown 8vo, 7s. 6d.

TACITUS.—The Agricola. A Translation. Small crown 8vo, 2s. 6d.

TARRING, *C. J.*—A Practical Elementary Turkish Grammar. Crown 8vo, 6s.

TAYLOR, *Hugh.*—The Morality of Nations. A Study in the Evolution of Ethics. Crown 8vo, 6s.

TAYLOR, *Rev. Canon Isaac, LL.D.*—The Alphabet. An Account of the Origin and Development of Letters. With numerous Tables and Facsimiles. 2 vols. Demy 8vo, 36s.

Leaves from an Egyptian Note-book. Crown 8vo.

TAYLOR, *Jeremy.*—The Marriage Ring. With Preface, Notes, and Appendices. Edited by FRANCIS BURDETT MONEY COUTTS. Small crown 8vo, 2s. 6d.

TAYLOR, *Reynell, C.B., C.S.I.* A Biography. By E. GAMBIER PARRY. With Portait and Map. Demy 8vo, 14s.

TAYLOR, *Sedley.*— Profit Sharing between Capital and Labour. To which is added a Memorandum on the Industrial Partnership at the Whitwood Collieries, by ARCHIBALD and HENRY BRIGGS, with remarks by SEDLEY TAYLOR. Crown 8vo, 2s. 6d.

THOM, *J. Hamilton.*—Laws of Life after the Mind of Christ. Two Series. Crown 8vo, 7s. 6d. each.

THOMPSON, *Sir H.*—Diet in Relation to Age and Activity. Fcap. 8vo, cloth, 1s. 6d. ; paper covers, 1s.

TIDMAN, *Paul F.*—Money and Labour. 1s. 6d.

TODHUNTER, *Dr. J.*—A Study of Shelley. Crown 8vo, 7s.

TOLSTOI, Count Leo.—Christ's Christianity. Translated from the Russian. Large crown 8vo, 7s. 6d.

TRANT, William.—Trade Unions; Their Origin, Objects, and Efficacy. Small crown 8vo, 1s. 6d.; paper covers, 1s.

TRENCH, The late R. C., Archbishop.—Letters and Memorials. By the Author of "Charles Lowder." With two Portraits. 2 vols. 8vo, 21s.

    Notes on the Parables of Our Lord. Fourteenth Edition. 8vo, 12s. Cheap Edition, 7s. 6d.

    Notes on the Miracles of Our Lord. Twelfth Edition. 8vo, 12s. Cheap Edition, 7s. 6d.

    Studies in the Gospels. Fifth Edition, Revised. 8vo, 10s. 6d.

    Brief Thoughts and Meditations on Some Passages in Holy Scripture. Third Edition. Crown 8vo, 3s. 6d.

    Synonyms of the New Testament. Tenth Edition, Enlarged. 8vo, 12s.

    Sermons New and Old. Crown 8vo, 6s.

    Westminster and other Sermons. Crown 8vo, 6s.

    On the Authorized Version of the New Testament. Second Edition. 8vo, 7s.

    Commentary on the Epistles to the Seven Churches in Asia. Fourth Edition, Revised. 8vo, 8s. 6d.

    The Sermon on the Mount. An Exposition drawn from the Writings of St. Augustine, with an Essay on his Merits as an Interpreter of Holy Scripture. Fourth Edition, Enlarged. 8vo, 10s. 6d.

    Shipwrecks of Faith. Three Sermons preached before the University of Cambridge in May, 1867. Fcap. 8vo, 2s. 6d.

    Lectures on Mediæval Church History. Being the Substance of Lectures delivered at Queen's College, London. Second Edition. 8vo, 12s.

    English, Past and Present. Thirteenth Edition, Revised and Improved. Fcap. 8vo, 5s.

    On the Study of Words. Twentieth Edition, Revised. Fcap. 8vo, 5s.

    Select Glossary of English Words Used Formerly in Senses Different from the Present. Sixth Edition, Revised and Enlarged. Fcap. 8vo, 5s.

    Proverbs and Their Lessons. Seventh Edition, Enlarged. Fcap. 8vo, 4s.

    Poems. Collected and Arranged anew. Ninth Edition. Fcap. 8vo, 7s. 6d.

TRENCH, *The late R. C., Archbishop.*—*continued.*

    Poems. Library Edition. 2 vols. Small crown 8vo, 10s.

    Sacred Latin Poetry. Chiefly Lyrical, Selected and Arranged for Use. Third Edition, Corrected and Improved. Fcap. 8vo, 7s.

    A Household Book of English Poetry. Selected and Arranged, with Notes. Fourth Edition, Revised. Extra fcap. 8vo, 5s. 6d.

    An Essay on the Life and Genius of Calderon. With Translations from his "Life's a Dream" and "Great Theatre of the World." Second Edition, Revised and Improved. Extra fcap. 8vo, 5s. 6d.

    Gustavus Adolphus in Germany, and other Lectures on the Thirty Years' War. Third Edition, Enlarged. Fcap. 8vo, 4s.

    Plutarch: his Life, his Lives, and his Morals. Second Edition, Enlarged. Fcap. 8vo, 3s. 6d.

    Remains of the late Mrs. Richard Trench. Being Selections from her Journals, Letters, and other Papers. New and Cheaper Issue. With Portrait. 8vo, 6s.

TUTHILL, *C. A. H.*—Origin and Development of Christian Dogma. Crown 8vo.

TWINING, *Louisa.*—Workhouse Visiting and Management during Twenty-Five Years. Small crown 8vo, 2s.

Two Centuries of Irish History. By various Writers. Edited by Prof. J. BRYCE. Demy 8vo.

VAL d'EREMAO, *Rev. J. P.*—The Serpent of Eden. A Philological and Critical Essay. Crown 8vo, 4s. 6d.

VICARY, *J. Fulford.*—Saga Time. With Illustrations. Crown 8vo, 7s. 6d.

VOLCKXSOM, *E. W. v.*—Catechism of Elementary Modern Chemistry. Small crown 8vo, 3s.

WALPOLE, *Chas. George.*—A Short History of Ireland from the Earliest Times to the Union with Great Britain. With 5 Maps and Appendices. Third Edition. Crown 8vo, 6s.

Words of Jesus Christ taken from the Gospels. Small crown 8vo, 2s. 6d.

WARD, *Wilfrid.*—The Wish to Believe. A Discussion Concerning the Temper of Mind in which a reasonable Man should undertake Religious Inquiry. Small crown 8vo, 5s.

WARD, *William George, Ph.D.*—Essays on the Philosophy of Theism. Edited, with an Introduction, by WILFRID WARD. 2 vols. Demy 8vo, 21s.

WARTER, J. W.—**An Old Shropshire Oak.** 2 vols. Demy 8vo, 28s.

WEDMORE, Frederick.—**The Masters of Genre Painting.** With Sixteen Illustrations. Post 8vo, 7s. 6d.

WHITMAN, Sidney.—**Conventional Cant: its Results and Remedy.** Crown 8vo, 6s.

WHITNEY, Prof. William Dwight.—**Essentials of English Grammar, for the Use of Schools.** Second Edition. Crown 8vo, 3s. 6d.

WHITWORTH, George Clifford.—**An Anglo-Indian Dictionary:** a Glossary of Indian Terms used in English, and of such English or other Non-Indian Terms as have obtained special meanings in India. Demy 8vo, cloth, 12s.

WILSON, Mrs. R. F.—**The Christian Brothers.** Their Origin and Work. With a Sketch of the Life of their Founder, the Ven. JEAN BAPTISTE, de la Salle. Crown 8vo, 6s.

WOLTMANN, Dr. Alfred, and WOERMANN, Dr. Karl.—**History of Painting.** With numerous Illustrations. Medium 8vo. Vol. I. Painting in Antiquity and the Middle Ages. 28s.; bevelled boards, gilt leaves, 30s. Vol. II. The Painting of the Renascence. 42s.; bevelled boards, gilt leaves, 45s.

YOUMANS, Edward L., M.D.—**A Class Book of Chemistry,** on the Basis of the New System. With 200 Illustrations. Crown 8vo, 5s.

YOUMANS, Eliza A.—**First Book of Botany.** Designed to Cultivate the Observing Powers of Children. With 300 Engravings. New and Cheaper Edition. Crown 8vo, 2s. 6d.

THE INTERNATIONAL SCIENTIFIC SERIES.

I. **Forms of Water in Clouds and Rivers, Ice and Glaciers.** By J. Tyndall, LL.D., F.R.S. With 25 Illustrations. Ninth Edition. 5s.

II. **Physics and Politics**; or, Thoughts on the Application of the Principles of "Natural Selection" and "Inheritance" to Political Society. By Walter Bagehot. Eighth Edition. 5s.

III. **Foods.** By Edward Smith, M.D., LL.B., F.R.S. With numerous Illustrations. Ninth Edition. 5s.

IV. **Mind and Body:** the Theories of their Relation. By Alexander Bain, LL.D. With Four Illustrations. Eighth Edition. 5s.

V. **The Study of Sociology.** By Herbert Spencer. Thirteenth Edition. 5s.

VI. **The Conservation of Energy.** By Balfour Stewart, M.A., LL.D., F.R.S. With 14 Illustrations. Seventh Edition. 5s.

VII. **Animal Locomotion**; or Walking, Swimming, and Flying. By J. B. Pettigrew, M.D., F.R.S., etc. With 130 Illustrations. Third Edition. 5s.

VIII. **Responsibility in Mental Disease.** By Henry Maudsley, M.D. Fourth Edition. 5s.

IX. **The New Chemistry.** By Professor J. P. Cooke. With 31 Illustrations. Ninth Edition. 5s.

X. **The Science of Law.** By Professor Sheldon Amos. Sixth Edition. 5s.

XI. **Animal Mechanism**: a Treatise on Terrestrial and Aerial Locomotion. By Professor E. J. Marey. With 117 Illustrations. Third Edition. 5s.

XII. **The Doctrine of Descent and Darwinism.** By Professor Oscar Schmidt. With 26 Illustrations. Seventh Edition. 5s.

XIII. **The History of the Conflict between Religion and Science.** By J. W. Draper, M.D., LL.D. Twentieth Edition. 5s.

XIV. **Fungi**: their Nature, Influences, and Uses. By M. C. Cooke, M.A., LL.D. Edited by the Rev. M. J. Berkeley, M.A., F.L.S. With numerous Illustrations. Fourth Edition. 5s.

XV. **The Chemistry of Light and Photography.** By Dr. Hermann Vogel. With 100 Illustrations. Fifth Edition. 5s.

XVI. **The Life and Growth of Language.** By Professor William Dwight Whitney. Fifth Edition. 5s.

XVII. **Money and the Mechanism of Exchange.** By W. Stanley Jevons, M.A., F.R.S. Eighth Edition. 5s.

XVIII. **The Nature of Light.** With a General Account of Physical Optics. By Dr. Eugene Lommel. With 188 Illustrations and a Table of Spectra in Chromo-lithography. Fourth Edition. 5s.

XIX. **Animal Parasites and Messmates.** By P. J. Van Beneden. With 83 Illustrations. Third Edition. 5s.

XX. **On Fermentation.** By Professor Schützenberger. With 28 Illustrations. Fourth Edition. 5s.

XXI. **The Five Senses of Man.** By Professor Bernstein. With 91 Illustrations. Fifth Edition. 5s.

XXII. **The Theory of Sound in its Relation to Music.** By Professor Pietro Blaserna. With numerous Illustrations. Third Edition. 5s.

XXIII. **Studies in Spectrum Analysis.** By J. Norman Lockyer, F.R.S. With six photographic Illustrations of Spectra, and numerous engravings on Wood. Fourth Edition. 6s. 6d.

XXIV. **A History of the Growth of the Steam Engine.** By Professor R. H. Thurston. With numerous Illustrations. Fourth Edition. 5s.

XXV. **Education as a Science.** By Alexander Bain, LL.D. Sixth Edition. 5s.

XXVI. **The Human Species.** By Professor A. de Quatrefages. Fourth Edition. 5s.

XXVII. **Modern Chromatics.** With Applications to Art and Industry. By Ogden N. Rood. With 130 original Illustrations. Second Edition. 5s.

XXVIII. **The Crayfish**: an Introduction to the Study of Zoology. By Professor T. H. Huxley. With 82 Illustrations. Fourth Edition. 5s.

XXIX. **The Brain as an Organ of Mind.** By H. Charlton Bastian, M.D. With numerous Illustrations. Third Edition. 5s.

XXX. **The Atomic Theory.** By Prof. Wurtz. Translated by E. Cleminshaw, F.C.S. Fifth Edition. 5s.

XXXI. **The Natural Conditions of Existence as they affect Animal Life.** By Karl Semper. With 2 Maps and 106 Woodcuts. Third Edition. 5s.

XXXII. **General Physiology of Muscles and Nerves.** By Prof. J. Rosenthal. Third Edition. With 75 Illustrations. 5s.

XXXIII. **Sight**: an Exposition of the Principles of Monocular and Binocular Vision. By Joseph le Conte, LL.D. Second Edition. With 132 Illustrations. 5s.

XXXIV. **Illusions**: a Psychological Study. By James Sully. Third Edition. 5s.

XXXV. **Volcanoes: what they are and what they teach.** By Professor J. W. Judd, F.R.S. With 96 Illustrations on Wood. Fourth Edition. 5s.

XXXVI. **Suicide**: an Essay on Comparative Moral Statistics. By Prof. H. Morselli. Second Edition. With Diagrams. 5s.

XXXVII. **The Brain and its Functions.** By J. Luys. With Illustrations. Second Edition. 5s.

XXXVIII. **Myth and Science**: an Essay. By Tito Vignoli. Third Edition. With Supplementary Note. 5s.

XXXIX. **The Sun.** By Professor Young. With Illustrations. Third Edition. 5s.

XL. **Ants, Bees, and Wasps**: a Record of Observations on the Habits of the Social Hymenoptera. By Sir John Lubbock, Bart., M.P. With 5 Chromo-lithographic Illustrations. Eighth Edition. 5s.

XLI. **Animal Intelligence.** By G. J. Romanes, LL.D., F.R.S. Fourth Edition. 5s.

XLII. **The Concepts and Theories of Modern Physics.** By J. B. Stallo. Third Edition. 5s.

XLIII. **Diseases of Memory**; An Essay in the Positive Psychology. By Prof. Th. Ribot. Third Edition. 5s.

XLIV. **Man before Metals.** By N. Joly, with 148 Illustrations. Fourth Edition. 5s.

XLV. **The Science of Politics.** By Prof. Sheldon Amos. Third Edition. 5s.

XLVI. **Elementary Meteorology.** By Robert H. Scott. Fourth Edition. With Numerous Illustrations. 5s.

XLVII. **The Organs of Speech and their Application in the Formation of Articulate Sounds.** By Georg Hermann Von Meyer. With 47 Woodcuts. 5s.

XLVIII. **Fallacies.** A View of Logic from the Practical Side. By Alfred Sidgwick. Second Edition. 5s.

XLIX. **Origin of Cultivated Plants.** By Alphonse de Candolle. Second Edition. 5s.

L. **Jelly-Fish, Star-Fish, and Sea-Urchins.** Being a Research on Primitive Nervous Systems. By G. J. Romanes. With Illustrations. 5s.

LI. **The Common Sense of the Exact Sciences.** By the late William Kingdon Clifford. Second Edition. With 100 Figures. 5s.

LII. **Physical Expression: Its Modes and Principles.** By Francis Warner, M.D., F.R.C.P., Hunterian Professor of Comparative Anatomy and Physiology, R.C.S.E. With 50 Illustrations. 5s.

LIII. **Anthropoid Apes.** By Robert Hartmann. With 63 Illustrations. 5s.

LIV. **The Mammalia in their Relation to Primeval Times.** By Oscar Schmidt. With 51 Woodcuts. 5s.

LV. **Comparative Literature.** By H. Macaulay Posnett, LL.D. 5s.

LVI. **Earthquakes and other Earth Movements.** By Prof. John Milne. With 38 Figures. Second Edition. 5s.

LVII. **Microbes, Ferments, and Moulds.** By E. L. Trouessart. With 107 Illustrations. 5s.

LVIII. **Geographical and Geological Distribution of Animals.** By Professor A. Heilprin. With Frontispiece. 5s.

LIX. **Weather.** A Popular Exposition of the Nature of Weather Changes from Day to Day. By the Hon. Ralph Abercromby. Second Edition. With 96 Illustrations. 5s.

LX. **Animal Magnetism.** By Alfred Binet and Charles Féré. 5s.

LXI. **Manual of British Discomycetes,** with descriptions of all the Species of Fungi hitherto found in Britain included in the Family, and Illustrations of the Genera. By William Phillips, F.L.S. 5s.

LXII. **International Law.** With Materials for a Code of International Law. By Professor Leone Levi. 5s.

LXIII. **The Geological History of Plants.** By Sir J. William Dawson. With 80 Figures. 5s.

LXIV. **The Origin of Floral Structures through Insect and other Agencies.** By Rev. Prof. G. Henslow. With 88 Illustrations. 5s.

LXV. **On the Senses, Instincts, and Intelligence of Animals.** With special Reference to Insects. By Sir John Lubbock, Bart., M.P. 100 Illustrations. 5s.

MILITARY WORKS.

BRACKENBURY, Col. C. B., R.A. — **Military Handbooks for Regimental Officers.**

I. **Military Sketching and Reconnaissance.** By Col. F. J. Hutchison and Major H. G. MacGregor. Fifth Edition. With 16 Plates. Small crown 8vo, 4s.

II. **The Elements of Modern Tactics Practically applied to English Formations.** By Lieut.-Col. Wilkinson Shaw. Sixth Edition. With 25 Plates and Maps. Small crown 8vo, 9s.

III. **Field Artillery.** Its Equipment, Organization and Tactics. By Major Sisson C. Pratt, R.A. With 12 Plates. Third Edition. Small crown 8vo, 6s.

IV. **The Elements of Military Administration.** First Part: Permanent System of Administration. By Major J. W. Buxton. Small crown 8vo, 7s. 6d.

V. **Military Law:** Its Procedure and Practice. By Major Sisson C. Pratt, R.A. Third Edition. Revised. Small crown 8vo, 4s. 6d.

VI. **Cavalry in Modern War.** By Major-General F. Chenevix Trench. Small crown 8vo, 6s.

VII. **Field Works.** Their Technical Construction and Tactical Application. By the Editor, Col. C. B. Brackenbury, R.A. Small crown 8vo.

BROOKE, Major, C. K. — **A System of Field Training.** Small crown 8vo, cloth limp, 2s.

Campaign of Fredericksburg, November—December, 1862. A Study for Officers of Volunteers. By a Line Officer. With 5 Maps and Plans. Second Edition. Crown 8vo, 5s.

CLERY, C. Francis, Col.—**Minor Tactics.** With 26 Maps and Plans. Seventh Edition, Revised. Crown 8vo, 9s.

COLVILE, Lieut.-Col. C. F.—**Military Tribunals.** Sewed, 2s. 6d.

CRAUFURD, Capt. H. J.—**Suggestions for the Military Training of a Company of Infantry.** Crown 8vo, 1s. 6d.

HAMILTON, Capt. Ian, A.D.C.—**The Fighting of the Future.** 1s.

HARRISON, Col. R.—**The Officer's Memorandum Book for Peace and War.** Fourth Edition, Revised throughout. Oblong 32mo, red basil, with pencil, 3s. 6d.

Notes on Cavalry Tactics, Organisation, etc. By a Cavalry Officer. With Diagrams. Demy 8vo, 12s.

PARR, Col. H. Hallam, C.M.G.—**The Dress, Horses, and Equipment of Infantry and Staff Officers.** Crown 8vo, 1s.

Further Training and Equipment of Mounted Infantry. Crown 8vo, 1s.

SCHAW, Col. H.—**The Defence and Attack of Positions and Localities.** Third Edition, Revised and Corrected. Crown 8vo, 3s. 6d.

STONE, Capt. F. Gleadowe, R.A.—**Tactical Studies from the Franco-German War of 1870-71.** With 22 Lithographic Sketches and Maps. Demy 8vo, 10s. 6d.

WILKINSON, H. Spenser, Capt. 20th Lancashire R.V.—**Citizen Soldiers.** Essays towards the Improvement of the Volunteer Force. Crown 8vo, 2s. 6d.

POETRY.

ADAM OF ST. VICTOR.—**The Liturgical Poetry of Adam of St. Victor.** From the text of GAUTIER. With Translations into English in the Original Metres, and Short Explanatory Notes, by DIGBY S. WRANGHAM, M.A. 3 vols. Crown 8vo, printed on hand-made paper, boards, 21s.

ALEXANDER, William, D.D., Bishop of Derry.—**St. Augustine's Holiday,** and other Poems. Crown 8vo, 6s.

AUCHMUTY, A. C.—**Poems of English Heroism:** From Brunanburh to Lucknow; from Athelstan to Albert. Small crown 8vo, 1s. 6d.

BARNES, William.—**Poems of Rural Life,** in the Dorset Dialect. New Edition, complete in one vol. Crown 8vo, 6s.

BAYNES, Rev. Canon H. R.—**Home Songs for Quiet Hours.** Fourth and Cheaper Edition. Fcap. 8vo, cloth, 2s. 6d.

BEVINGTON, L. S.—**Key Notes.** Small crown 8vo, 5s.

BLUNT, Wilfrid Scawen.—**The Wind and the Whirlwind.** Demy 8vo, 1s. 6d.

 The Love Sonnets of Proteus. Fifth Edition, 18mo. Cloth extra, gilt top, 5s.

Book of Verse, A. By J. R. W. Small crown 8vo, 2s. 6d.

BOWEN, H. C., M.A.—**Simple English Poems.** English Literature for Junior Classes. In Four Parts. Parts I., II., and III., 6d. each, and Part IV., 1s. Complete, 3s.

BRYANT, W. C.—**Poems.** Cheap Edition, with Frontispiece. Small crown 8vo, 3s. 6d.

Calderon's Dramas: the Wonder-Working Magician—Life is a Dream—the Purgatory of St. Patrick. Translated by DENIS FLORENCE MACCARTHY. Post 8vo, 10s.

Camoens' Lusiads.—Portuguese Text, with Translation by J. J. AUBERTIN. Second Edition. 2 vols. Crown 8vo, 12s.

CAMPBELL, Lewis.—**Sophocles.** The Seven Plays in English Verse. Crown 8vo, 7s. 6d.

CHRISTIE, Albany J.—**The End of Man.** Fourth Edition. Fcap. 8vo, 2s. 6d.

COXHEAD, Ethel.—**Birds and Babies.** With 33 Illustrations. Imp. 16mo, 1s.

Dante's Divina Commedia. Translated in the *Terza Rima* of Original, by F. K. H. HASELFOOT. Demy 8vo, 16s.

DENNIS, J.—**English Sonnets.** Collected and Arranged by. Small crown 8vo, 2s. 6d.

DE VERE, Aubrey.—**Poetical Works.**
 I. THE SEARCH AFTER PROSERPINE, etc. 6s.
 II. THE LEGENDS OF ST. PATRICK, etc. 6s.
 III. ALEXANDER THE GREAT, etc. 6s.

 The Foray of Queen Meave, and other Legends of Ireland's Heroic Age. Small crown 8vo, 5s.

 Legends of the Saxon Saints. Small crown 8vo, 6s.

 Legends and Records of the Church and the Empire. Small crown 8vo, 6s.

DOBSON, Austin.—**Old World Idylls** and other Verses. Eighth Edition. Elzevir 8vo, gilt top, 6s.

At the Sign of the Lyre. Fifth Edition. Elzevir 8vo, gilt top, 6s.

Dorica. By E. D. S. Small crown 8vo, 5s.

DOWDEN, Edward, LL.D.—**Shakspere's Sonnets.** With Introduction and Notes. Large post 8vo, 7s. 6d.

DUTT, Toru.—**A Sheaf Gleaned in French Fields.** New Edition. Demy 8vo, 10s. 6d.

Ancient Ballads and Legends of Hindustan. With an Introductory Memoir by EDMUND GOSSE. Second Edition, 18mo. Cloth extra, gilt top, 5s.

ELLIOTT, Ebenezer, The Corn Law Rhymer.—**Poems.** Edited by his son, the Rev. EDWIN ELLIOTT, of St. John's, Antigua. 2 vols. Crown 8vo, 18s.

English Verse. Edited by W. J. LINTON and R. H. STODDARD. 5 vols. Crown 8vo, cloth, 5s. each.
- I. CHAUCER TO BURNS.
- II. TRANSLATIONS.
- III. LYRICS OF THE NINETEENTH CENTURY.
- IV. DRAMATIC SCENES AND CHARACTERS.
- V. BALLADS AND ROMANCES.

GOSSE, Edmund.—**New Poems.** Crown 8vo, 7s. 6d.

Firdausi in Exile, and other Poems. Second Edition. Elzevir 8vo, gilt top, 6s.

GURNEY, Rev. Alfred.—**The Vision of the Eucharist,** and other Poems. Crown 8vo, 5s.

A Christmas Faggot. Small crown 8vo, 5s.

HAMILTON, Ian.—**The Ballad of Hadji,** and other Poems. With Frontispiece and Vignettes. Elzevir 8vo, 3s. 6d.

HARRISON, Clifford.—**In Hours of Leisure.** Second Edition. Crown 8vo, 5s.

HEYWOOD, J. C.—**Herodias,** a Dramatic Poem. New Edition, Revised. Small crown 8vo, 5s.

Antonius. A Dramatic Poem. New Edition, Revised. Small crown 8vo, 5s.

Salome. A Dramatic Poem. Small crown 8vo, 5s.

HICKEY, E. H.—**A Sculptor,** and other Poems. Small crown 8vo, 5s.

KEATS, John.—**Poetical Works.** Edited by W. T. ARNOLD. Large crown 8vo, choicely printed on hand-made paper, with Portrait in *eau-forte*. Parchment or cloth, 12s.; vellum, 15s. New Edition, crown 8vo, cloth, 3s. 6d.

KING, *Mrs. Hamilton.*—The Disciples. Ninth Edition. Small crown 8vo, 5s.; Elzevir Edition, cloth extra, 6s.
  A Book of Dreams. Third Edition. Crown 8vo, 3s. 6d.
  The Sermon in the Hospital (From "The Disciples"). Fcap. 8vo, 1s. Cheap Edition for distribution 3d., or 20s. per 100.

LANG, A.—XXXII. Ballades in Blue China. Elzevir 8vo, 5s.
  Rhymes à la Mode. With Frontispiece by E. A. Abbey. Second Edition. Elzevir 8vo, cloth extra, gilt top, 5s.

LAWSON, *Right Hon. Mr. Justice.*—Hymni Usitati Latine Redditi: with other Verses. Small 8vo, parchment, 5s.

Living English Poets MDCCCLXXXII. With Frontispiece by Walter Crane. Second Edition. Large crown 8vo. Printed on hand-made paper. Parchment or cloth, 12s.; vellum, 15s.

LOCKER, F.—London Lyrics. Tenth Edition. With Portrait, Elzevir 8vo. Cloth extra, gilt top, 5s.

Love in Idleness. A Volume of Poems. With an Etching by W. B. Scott. Small crown 8vo, 5s.

MAGNUSSON, *Eirikr, M.A., and* PALMER, *E. H., M.A.*—Johan Ludvig Runeberg's Lyrical Songs, Idylls, and Epigrams. Fcap. 8vo, 5s.

Matin Songs. Small crown 8vo, 2s.

MEREDITH, *Owen [The Earl of Lytton].*—Lucile. New Edition. With 32 Illustrations. 16mo, 3s. 6d. Cloth extra, gilt edges, 4s. 6d.

MORRIS, *Lewis.*—Poetical Works of. New and Cheaper Editions, with Portrait. Complete in 3 vols., 5s. each.
  Vol. I. contains "Songs of Two Worlds." Twelfth Edition.
  Vol. II. contains "The Epic of Hades." Twenty-second Edition.
  Vol. III. contains "Gwen" and "The Ode of Life." Seventh Edition.
  Vol. IV. contains "Songs Unsung" and "Gycia." Fifth Edition.
  Songs of Britain. Third Edition. Fcap. 8vo, 5s.
  The Epic of Hades. With 16 Autotype Illustrations, after the Drawings of the late George R. Chapman. 4to, cloth extra, gilt leaves, 21s.
  The Epic of Hades. Presentation Edition. 4to, cloth extra, gilt leaves, 10s. 6d.
  The Lewis Morris Birthday Book. Edited by S. S. Copeman, with Frontispiece after a Design by the late George R. Chapman. 32mo, cloth extra, gilt edges, 2s.; cloth limp, 1s. 6d.

MORSHEAD, *E. D. A.*—The House of Atreus. Being the Agamemnon, Libation-Bearers, and Furies of Æschylus. Translated into English Verse. Crown 8vo, 7s.

MORSHEAD, E. D. A.—continued.
   The Suppliant Maidens of Æschylus. Crown 8vo, 3s. 6d.
MULHOLLAND, Rosa.—Vagrant Verses. Small crown 8vo, 5s.
NADEN, Constance C. W.—A Modern Apostle, and other Poems. Small crown 8vo, 5s.
NOEL, The Hon. Roden.—A Little Child's Monument. Third Edition. Small crown 8vo, 3s. 6d.
   The House of Ravensburg. New Edition. Small crown 8vo, 6s.
   The Red Flag, and other Poems. New Edition. Small crown 8vo, 6s.
   Songs of the Heights and Deeps. Crown 8vo, 6s.
O'HAGAN, John.—The Song of Roland. Translated into English Verse. New and Cheaper Edition. Crown 8vo, 5s.
PFEIFFER, Emily.—The Rhyme of the Lady of the Rock, and How it Grew. Second Edition. Small crown 8vo, 3s. 6d.
   Gerard's Monument, and other Poems. Second Edition. Crown 8vo, 6s.
   Under the Aspens: Lyrical and Dramatic. With Portrait. Crown 8vo, 6s.
Rare Poems of the 16th and 17th Centuries. Edited by W. J. LINTON. Crown 8vo, 5s.
RHOADES, James.—The Georgics of Virgil. Translated into English Verse. Small crown 8vo, 5s.
   Poems. Small crown 8vo, 4s. 6d.
   Dux Redux. A Forest Tangle. Small crown 8vo, 3s. 6d.
ROBINSON, A. Mary F.—A Handful of Honeysuckle. Fcap. 8vo, 3s. 6d.
   The Crowned Hippolytus. Translated from Euripides. With New Poems. Small crown 8vo, 5s.
SCOTT, Fredk. George.—The Soul's Quest. Small crown 8vo.
SHARP, Isaac.—Saul of Tarsus, and other Poems. Small crown 8vo, 2s. 6d.
SMITH, J. W. Gilbart.—The Loves of Vandyck. A Tale of Genoa. Small crown 8vo, 2s. 6d.
   The Log o' the "Norseman." Small crown 8vo, 5s.
   Serbelloni. Small crown 8vo, 5s.
Sophocles: The Seven Plays in English Verse. Translated by LEWIS CAMPBELL. Crown 8vo, 7s. 6d.

Kegan Paul, Trench & Co.'s Publications. 39

SYMONDS, *John Addington.*—Vagabunduli Libellus. Crown 8vo, 6s.

Tasso's Jerusalem Delivered. Translated by Sir JOHN KINGSTON JAMES, Bart. Two Volumes. Printed on hand-made paper, parchment, bevelled boards. Large crown 8vo, 21s.

TAYLOR, *Sir H.*—Works. Complete in Five Volumes. Crown 8vo, 30s.
    Philip Van Artevelde. Fcap. 8vo, 3s. 6d.
    The Virgin Widow, etc. Fcap. 8vo, 3s. 6d.

TODHUNTER, *Dr. J.*—Laurella, and other Poems. Crown 8vo, 6s. 6d.
    Forest Songs. Small crown 8vo, 3s. 6d.
    The True Tragedy of Rienzi: a Drama. 3s. 6d.
    Alcestis: a Dramatic Poem. Extra fcap. 8vo, 5s.
    Helena in Troas. Small crown 8vo, 2s. 6d.
    The Banshee, and other Poems. Small crown 8vo, 3s. 6d.

TYNAN, *Katherine.*—Louise de la Valliere, and other Poems. Small crown 8vo, 3s. 6d.
    Shamrocks. Small crown 8vo, 5s.

TYRER, *C. E.*—Fifty Sonnets. Small crown 8vo, 1s. 6d.

Victorian Hymns: English Sacred Songs of Fifty Years. Dedicated to the Queen. Large post 8vo, 10s. 6d.

WILLIS, *E. Cooper, Q.C.*—Tales and Legends in Verse. Small crown 8vo, 3s. 6d.

Wordsworth Birthday Book, The. Edited by ADELAIDE and VIOLET WORDSWORTH. 32mo, limp cloth, 1s. 6d.; cloth extra, 2s.

NOVELS AND TALES.

BANKS, *Mrs. G. L.* God's Providence House. Crown 8vo, 6s.

MICHELE, *Mary.*—Doing and Undoing. A Story. Crown 8vo, 4s. 6d.

CRAWFURD, *Oswald.*—Sylvia Arden. With Frontispiece. Crown 8vo, 6s.

GARDINER, *Linda.*—His Heritage. With Frontispiece. Crown 8vo, 6s.

GRAY, *Maxwell.*—The Silence of Dean Maitland. Fifteenth thousand. With Frontispiece. Crown 8vo, 6s.

GREY, *Rowland.*—In Sunny Switzerland. A Tale of Six Weeks. Second Edition. Small crown 8vo, 5s.

GREY, Rowland.—continued.
    Lindenblumen and other Stories. Small crown 8vo, 5s.
    By Virtue of his Office. Crown 8vo, 6s.

HUNTER, Hay.—The Crime of Christmas Day. A Tale of the Latin Quarter. By the Author of "My Ducats and my Daughter." 1s.

HUNTER, Hay, and WHYTE, Walter.—My Ducats and My Daughter. With Frontispiece. Crown 8vo, 6s.

INGELOW, Jean.—Off the Skelligs: a Novel. With Frontispiece. Crown 8vo, 6s.

JENKINS, Edward.—A Secret of Two Lives. Crown 8vo, 2s. 6d.

KIELLAND, Alexander L.—Garman and Worse. A Norwegian Novel. Authorized Translation, by W. W. Kettlewell. Crown 8vo, 6s.

LANG, Andrew.—In the Wrong Paradise, and other Stories. Crown 8vo, 6s.

MACDONALD, G.—Donal Grant. A Novel. With Frontispiece. Crown 8vo, 6s.

    Home Again. With Frontispiece. Crown 8vo, 6s.
    Castle Warlock. A Novel. With Frontispiece. Crown 8vo, 6s.
    Malcolm. With Portrait of the Author engraved on Steel. Crown 8vo, 6s.
    The Marquis of Lossie. With Frontispiece. Crown 8vo, 6s.
    St. George and St. Michael. With Frontispiece. Crown 8vo, 6s.
    What's Mine's Mine. With Frontispiece. Crown 8vo, 6s.
    Annals of a Quiet Neighbourhood. With Frontispiece. Crown 8vo, 6s.
    The Seaboard Parish: a Sequel to "Annals of a Quiet Neighbourhood." With Frontispiece. Crown 8vo, 6s.
    Wilfred Cumbermede. An Autobiographical Story. With Frontispiece. Crown 8vo, 6s.
    Thomas Wingfold, Curate. With Frontispiece. Crown 8vo, 6s.
    Paul Faber, Surgeon. With Frontispiece. Crown 8vo, 6s.
    The Elect Lady. With Frontispiece. Crown 8vo, 6s.

MALET, Lucas.—Colonel Enderby's Wife. A Novel. With Frontispiece. Crown 8vo, 6s.
    A Counsel of Perfection. With Frontispiece. Crown 8vo, 6s.

MULHOLLAND, *Rosa.*—Marcella Grace. An Irish Novel. Crown 8vo. 6s.

OGLE, *Anna C.*—A Lost Love. Small crown 8vo, 2s. 6d.

PALGRAVE, *W. Gifford.*—Hermann Agha: an Eastern Narrative. Crown 8vo, 6s.

Romance of the Recusants. By the Author of "Life of a Prig." Crown 8vo, 5s.

SEVERNE, *Florence.*—The Pillar House. With Frontispiece. Crown 8vo, 6s.

SHAW, *Flora L.*—Castle Blair: a Story of Youthful Days. Crown 8vo, 3s. 6d.

STRETTON, *Hesba.*—Through a Needle's Eye: a Story. With Frontispiece. Crown 8vo, 6s.

TAYLOR, *Col. Meadows, C.S.I., M.R.I.A.*—Seeta: a Novel. With Frontispiece. Crown 8vo, 6s.

    Tippoo Sultaun: a Tale of the Mysore War. With Frontispiece. Crown 8vo, 6s.

    Ralph Darnell. With Frontispiece. Crown 8vo, 6s.

    A Noble Queen. With Frontispiece. Crown 8vo, 6s.

    The Confessions of a Thug. With Frontispiece. Crown 8vo, 6s.

    Tara: a Mahratta Tale. With Frontispiece. Crown 8vo, 6s.

Within Sound of the Sea. With Frontispiece. Crown 8vo, 6s.

BOOKS FOR THE YOUNG.

Brave Men's Footsteps. A Book of Example and Anecdote for Young People. By the Editor of "Men who have Risen." With 4 Illustrations by C. Doyle. Ninth Edition. Crown 8vo, 2s. 6d.

COXHEAD, *Ethel.*—Birds and Babies. With 33 Illustrations. Second Edition. Imp. 16mo, cloth, 1s.

DAVIES, *G. Christopher.*—Rambles and Adventures of our School Field Club. With 4 Illustrations. New and Cheaper Edition. Crown 8vo, 3s. 6d.

EDMONDS, *Herbert.*—Well Spent Lives: a Series of Modern Biographies. New and Cheaper Edition. Crown 8vo, 3s. 6d.

EVANS, *Mark.*—The Story of our Father's Love, told to Children. Sixth and Cheaper Edition of Theology for Children. With 4 Illustrations. Fcap. 8vo, 1s. 6d.

MAC KENNA, *S. J.*—Plucky Fellows. A Book for Boys. With 6 Illustrations. Fifth Edition. Crown 8vo, 3s. 6d.

MALET, Lucas.—**Little Peter.** A Christmas Morality for Children of any Age. With numerous Illustrations. Fourth thousand. 5*s*.

REANEY, Mrs. G. S.—**Waking and Working;** or, From Girlhood to Womanhood. New and Cheaper Edition. With a Frontispiece. Crown 8vo, 3*s*. 6*d*.

   Blessing and Blessed: a Sketch of Girl Life. New and Cheaper Edition. Crown 8vo, 3*s*. 6*d*.

   Rose Gurney's Discovery. A Story for Girls. Dedicated to their Mothers. Crown 8vo, 3*s*. 6*d*.

   English Girls: Their Place and Power. With Preface by the Rev. R. W. Dale. Fifth Edition. Fcap. 8vo, 2*s*. 6*d*.

   Just Anyone, and other Stories. Three Illustrations. Royal 16mo, 1*s*. 6*d*.

   Sunbeam Willie, and other Stories. Three Illustrations. Royal 16mo, 1*s*. 6*d*.

   Sunshine Jenny, and other Stories. Three Illustrations. Royal 16mo, 1*s*. 6*d*.

STORR, Francis, and TURNER, Hawes.—**Canterbury Chimes;** or, Chaucer Tales re-told to Children. With 6 Illustrations from the Ellesmere Manuscript. Third Edition. Fcap. 8vo, 3*s*. 6*d*.

STRETTON, Hesba.—**David Lloyd's Last Will.** With 4 Illustrations. New Edition. Royal 16mo, 2*s*. 6*d*.

WHITAKER, Florence.—**Christy's Inheritance.** A London Story. Illustrated. Royal 16mo, 1*s*. 6*d*.

THE PARCHMENT LIBRARY EDITION.

THE AVON EDITION.

The Text of these Editions is mainly that of Delius. Wherever a variant reading is adopted, some good and recognized Shaksperian Critic has been followed. In no case is a new rendering of the text proposed; nor has it been thought necessary to distract the reader's attention by notes or comments.

SHAKSPERE'S WORKS.

THE AVON EDITION.

Printed on thin opaque paper, and forming 12 handy volumes, cloth, 18s., or bound in 6 volumes, 15s.

The set of 12 volumes may also be had in a cloth box, price 21s., or bound in Roan, Persian, Crushed Persian Levant, Calf, or Morocco, and enclosed in an attractive leather box at prices from 31s. 6d. upwards.

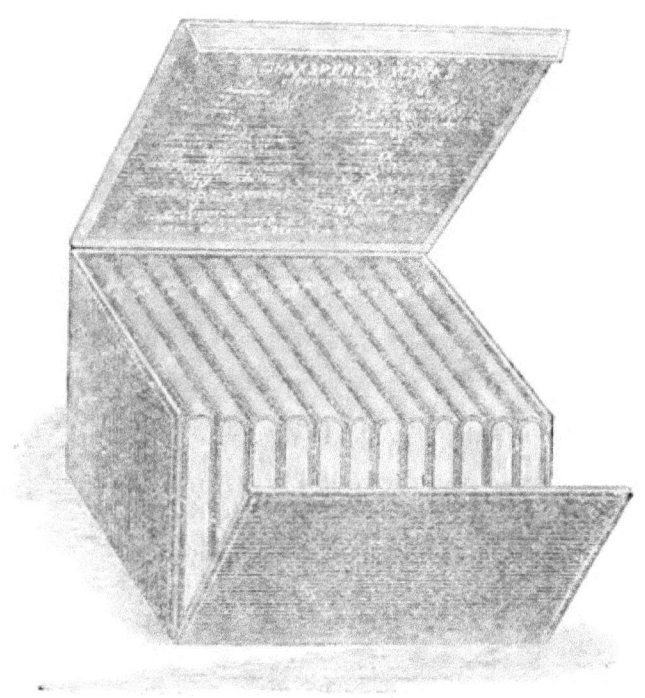

SOME PRESS NOTICES.

"This edition will be useful to those who want a good text, well and clearly printed, in convenient little volumes that will slip easily into an overcoat pocket or a travelling-bag."—*St. James's Gazette.*

"We know no prettier edition of Shakspere for the price."—*Academy.*

"It is refreshing to meet with an edition of Shakspere of convenient size and low price, without either notes or introductions of any sort to distract the attention of the reader."—*Saturday Review.*

"It is exquisite. Each volume is handy, is beautifully printed, and in every way lends itself to the taste of the cultivated student of Shakspere."—*Scotsman.*

THE PARCHMENT LIBRARY EDITION.

In 12 volumes Elzevir 8vo., choicely printed on hand-made paper, and bound in parchment or cloth, price £3 12s., or in vellum, price £4 10s.

The set of 12 volumes may also be had in a strong cloth box, price £3 17s., or with an oak hanging shelf, £3 18s.

SOME PRESS NOTICES.

" . . . There is, perhaps, no edition in which the works of Shakspere can be read in such luxury of type and quiet distinction of form as this, and we warmly recommend it."—*Pall Mall Gazette.*

"For elegance of form and beauty of typography, no edition of Shakspere hitherto published has excelled the 'Parchment Library Edition.' . . . They are in the strictest sense pocket volumes, yet the type is bold, and, being on fine white hand-made paper, can hardly tax the weakest of sight. The print is judiciously confined to the text, notes being more appropriate to library editions. The whole will be comprised in the cream-coloured parchment which gives the name to the series."—*Daily News.*

"The Parchment Library Edition of Shakspere needs no further praise." *Saturday Review.*

Just published. Price 5s.

AN INDEX TO THE WORKS OF SHAKSPERE.

Applicable to all editions of Shakspere, and giving reference, by topics, to notable passages and significant expressions; brief histories of the plays; geographical names and historic incidents; mention of all characters and sketches of important ones; together with explanations of allusions and obscure and obsolete words and phrases.

By EVANGELINE M. O'CONNOR.

LONDON: KEGAN PAUL, TRENCH & CO., 1, PATERNOSTER SQUARE.

SHAKSPERE'S WORKS.

SPECIMEN OF TYPE.

Salar. My wind, cooling my broth,
Would blow me to an ague, when I thought
What harm a wind too great might do at sea.
I should not see the sandy hour-glass run
But I should think of shallows and of flats,
And see my wealthy Andrew, dock'd in sand,
Vailing her high-top lower than her ribs
To kiss her burial. Should I go to church
And see the holy edifice of stone,
And not bethink me straight of dangerous rocks,
Which touching but my gentle vessel's side,
Would scatter all her spices on the stream,
Enrobe the roaring waters with my silks,
And, in a word, but even now worth this,
And now worth nothing? Shall I have the thought
To think on this, and shall I lack the thought
That such a thing bechanc'd would make me sad?
But tell not me: I know Antonio
Is sad to think upon his merchandise.
 Ant. Believe me, no: I thank my fortune for it,
My ventures are not in one bottom trusted,
Nor to one place; nor is my whole estate
Upon the fortune of this present year:
Therefore my merchandise makes me not sad.
 Salar. Why, then you are in love.
 Ant. Fie, fie!
 Salar. Not in love neither? Then let us say you
 are sad,
Because you are not merry; and 'twere as easy
For you to laugh, and leap, and say you are merry,
Because you are not sad. Now, by two-headed
 Janus,
Nature hath fram'd strange fellows in her time:
Some that will evermore peep through their eyes
And laugh like parrots at a bag-piper;
And other of such vinegar aspect

www.ingramcontent.com/pod-product-compliance
Lightning Source LLC
Chambersburg PA
CBHW031335160426
43196CB00007B/695